ALL THE CATHOLIC PEOPLE

ALL THE
CATHOLIC PEOPLE

Where Did All the Spirit Go?

MICHAEL NOVAK

HERDER AND HERDER

1971
HERDER AND HERDER NEW YORK
232 Madison Avenue, New York 10016

Library of Congress Catalog Card Number: 76–165498
© 1971 by Herder and Herder, Inc.
Manufactured in the United States

Contents

Acknowledgements

I am grateful to the following publishers for permission to reprint, in revised, expanded or altered form, the following material:

to *Commonweal* for "Where Did All the Spirit Go?"; some paragraphs from "On Being a Catholic" (chapter six); "Gimme is Dead" (chapter nine);

to Fortress Press for "Honesty and Freedom," from *Intellectual Honesty and Religious Commitment,* edited by Arthur J. Bellinzoni, Jr. and Thomas V. Litzenburg, Jr. (chapter two);

to *The National Catholic Reporter* for "All the Catholic People," "Picking and Choosing," and "Distinctive Traits";

to *Commentary* for a version of the passages on Maritain (chapter six);

to *Psychology Today* (© Communications/Research/Machines, Inc.) for some of the paragraphs in chapter seven;

to *Una Sancta* for "Reflections on Style";

to *Theology Today* for "What is Theology's Standpoint?" (chapter ten);

to *Christianity and Crisis* for "Planetary Theology" (chapter eleven);

to *The Center* for "The Enlightenment is Dead" (chapter twelve).

Chapters thirteen and fourteen appear here for the first time. I have had this book in mind for years, patiently accumulating chapters as time and occasion allowed.

Judy Lally helped me in the final stages, Carol Christ in the earlier stages, of criticizing and re-writing. Margie Geib read proofs.

For George and Helen Minno
warm friends
and
strong encouragers when I was young

Introduction

WAS there really a "melting pot" in America? Many of us have remained different from one another, different in instinct, emphasis, manner, priorities, imagination. Is it because of something in our genes? Were we too long nourished on potatoes, or pasta, or poppyseed, or bagels? Was it simply the weight of a thousand-year tradition, the accumulated family style nurtured in a chain of generations? Whatever the cause, groups among us are infuriated by values that others cherish; are attracted by what others find repellent; have criteria for judgment others disdain; find delight—and are bored—at different places. We value children differently. Our attitudes toward women, ambition, anger, and irrationality diverge.

Intermarriage and mobility have rendered our ethnic, religious, and racial traditions weaker, confused, and often qualified. Still, it is amazing how various this nation is, how differently the language is used from group to group, how delicately diverse are community points of view. The dominance of the national liberal culture in the universities and the media has obscured these differences during the last twenty years. But every practical politician, community organizer, and student of variety learns to modulate his perceptions, instincts, language, and judgments as he tries to meet our different concrete communities on their own terms. The nation is rediscovering its pluralism.

Events have driven me back again and again (I did not really want to get away) to recognize that to be a Catholic is to be neither a Jew nor a Protestant, whether of the classical or of the evangelical temperament. To be a Catholic is in a thousand subtle ways to be different from others. It is so, even if one "ceases to be a Catholic." (Only of Catholics does one ask whether they are "practicing." "Are you a practicing Protestant?" isn't a significant question. "Practicing atheist" is odd. "Believing Jew"?

There is a Catholic sensibility. (There are several such: a set of family resemblances). If sociologists cannot find it, let us shrug at the grossness of their tools: a fairly mediocre lot, on the whole, as their speech reveals. Watch Catholics deal with the demands made by a large family; with death; with tragedy; with authority figures; with political actions. Catholics by and large have a different style. Stating the differences is more difficult than living them; more difficult, even, than becoming slowly and vividly aware of them.

Why should we nourish such differences? Perhaps we shouldn't. Every day one meets men and women of intellectual distinction and refined sensibility who have "outgrown" their Catholic days. They are building an enlightened family culture in which to raise their children: somewhat leftward, universalist, the opposite (they hope) of parochial. But it is quite likely that the enlightenment is dead, and that the national liberal culture—the "constituency of conscience" to which liberal Senators appeal—is itself a small cultural pocket in the planetary scheme. It has some of the resources, not nearly enough, for imagining how to protect diversity upon this globe.

For one thing, the national liberal culture tends to be missionary. Despite protests, its base lies in reason, science, and technology. Despite its romantic wing, its power lies in the intellectual skills required to live with technology. It has a strong tendency toward homogeneity. Its mission is to "enlighten" the whole planet. Its conception of conscience attaches "right" and "just" to what is universal, not to what is local, living, and concrete. Hence, the impetus it gives to "civil rights," "equality," and

12

"reform" or even "revolution." It tends to impose these values on local populations, whether inwardly they desire such values or not. (The U.S. is in Vietnam for the "self-determination" of the Vietnamese.)

For another thing, the national liberal culture has at its core a fateful contradiction. One of its ideals moves toward universal order: world stability sufficient for long-range planning. Its contradictory ideal is the cult of the individual. Fulfillment lies (it teaches) in "liberation" from social "repression"—in doing what one wishes when one wishes. Thus, one of its goals is total self-expression; another is universal harmony through reason. In the sphere of the individual, it tends to encourage impulses, fantasies, the non-rational, the zany, the uninhibited, the exciting. In the sphere of the social, it tends to emphasize due process, compromise, efficiency, order, channelling. On the one hand, total planning; on the other hand, spontaneity.[1] The model implicit behind the national liberal culture in the days of its disintegration remains the model of its birth: utilitarianism. "Do what you wish so long as it does not harm others." *Laissez-faire.* "Do your thing." Liberalism, conservatism, and radicalism are variations on a single national theme.

Catholicism has taken up residence with many other kinds of culture. There is no *a priori* reason to believe that modern culture is less worthy than Byzantine or medieval Roman culture. But

[1] Marshall Berman writes: "The idea that I have called 'the politics of authenticity' is a dream of an ideal community in which individuality will not be subsumed and sacrificed, but fully developed and expressed. This dream is at once old and new. 'New,' first of all, in that it is modern: it presupposes the sort of fluid, highly mobile, urban society, and the sort of dynamic, expansive economy, which we experience as distinctively modern, and which nearly everyone in the West lives in today. But it is 'old' too: it has been a leitmotif in Western culture since early in the eighteenth century . . ." *The Politics of Authenticity,* New York, 1970, p. ix.

it would be a mistake to believe that the Catholic people will find a permanent resting place in modern liberal culture. Much that modern culture gives witness to is new in world history; much is admirable; much is to be rejected. The Catholic, insofar as his chief identity is transtemporal and transcultural in scope, both gives himself to and reserves part of himself from liberal culture. He is identified with more than one culture; with an historical people of more than one era. He lives incarnated within one given culture, but is not wholly defined thereby.

That it should be so is, perhaps, plain: the injunction to be "in the world but not of it" is classical. That it is so in fact is almost equally plain. Few are the Catholics who in their family traditions, their childrearing practices, their neighborhoods, their singing of ancient hymns and attendance at centuries-old mysteries have not learned to love aspects of cultures of the past, and are not thereby fortified against a wholehearted embrace of the present. To be sure, Catholics are not alone in cherishing cultural memories. For many men, little is of greater value than the living past. The forces of modern relevance and liberal enlightenment often grow weary, for they must extirpate ("*Ecrasez l'infame!*") what they call prejudices, customs, traditions, myths, superstitions, and predilections. But others call some among such matters roots. How does one pull the weeds and save the wheat?

As always, a Catholic struggles on many fronts at once. Today, his own faith is a problem to him, almost surely the primary problem. Why should he believe in God at all? Why continue to belong to the church? These questions are in the most pressing way practical: How shall he bring up his children? What shall he do with his own moral energies? It is possible that to help the Catholic Church is to retard among men the advance of justice, truth, charity, and freedom. It is possible that to be a Catholic

14

is positively harmful; or perhaps a profligate expenditure of labor. Many good persons during the past two decades have come to think so.

With cultural conservatives, liberals, and radicals, the Catholic also tends to have various and shifting arguments. The issues do not hold still; the contexts are not fixed. If at times he seems to side with radicals against liberals, or liberals against conservatives, or conservatives against radicals and liberals, it is probably because he is not, in fact, entirely at home within American culture. He brings to American culture instincts and criteria which, in the round, it seldom satisfies. Coalitions come and go; symbols change; motives, causes, and consequences shift. He desperately requires flexibility, intelligence, discrimination. "Discernment of spirits" is the gift for which he thirsts. No one party, cause, or cultural force can for too long hold his allegiance, not because he is a distinct individual solely, but because he belongs to a distinctive people. The source of his judgments is communal as well as personal.

Living as a Catholic, with integrity, in these times—perhaps it cannot be done. Perhaps it is not worth the effort. The chapters of this book are an attempt to accept that risk and to face its implications.

What I write here is not separable from what I have written elsewhere; my work, although not systematic in some geometric or logical sense, is of a piece. The natural rhythm of the human mind, which I prefer to follow, has its own inexorable dialectic: a step here, a pause there, a retreat, a breakthrough, an exploration, a consolidation. Thus the chapters here assembled record an abiding interest and exercise of mine: an attempt to comprehend the restlessness I feel at being born Catholic. Often I feel quiet gratitude; often despair at the encrustations that hide, distort, and destroy the vital life of my people; occasionally hope that we shall look ahead and be as creative as our forebears were, inventing as they invented.

I sense in my bones the despair at modern industrial democracy expressed with so much biting wit by Evelyn Waugh. (A Marxist doctoral candidate at Stanford taught me to compare Waugh's critique of industrial England point-by-point with Marx.) In many ways, I would like to call myself a conservative. But in the United States the word seems to mean uncritical, flippant, and very rich; in England it appears to require gout. I find no label apt. Slowly I stake out a path of concern: about the God in whom we live, who speaks to us through events; about institutions, shaped by different necessities and in a different time and now requiring transformation; about what constitutes personal development in a technological time. *Where shall we turn? What will become of us? What should we do?*

Elsewhere, I have defined theology as "the study of ultimate visions of communal relationships and personal identity, insofar as these affect actual human experience." This short book, then, is an essay in theology—close to experience, close to the concerns of many, and in its own plodding way "systematic." It belongs, perhaps, to that specialty of theology which Lonergan calls "communications," most closely related to my work in "dialectics" and "foundations." These are, if not the most esteemed specialties among professionals in the field, nevertheless among the most fertile, creative, and delightful to practice. They *do* stay quite close to the thickness of life, its lived experiences, its textures, its irrational and unpredictable contours—and that is where I should wish, when all is said, to be found.

Bayville, Long Island
June, 1971

ALL THE CATHOLIC PEOPLE

1

Where Did All the Spirit Go?

I REMEMBER well the feeling of exhilaration in Rome some years ago, the night of the climactic vote on collegiality. The moon over St. Peter's Square was brilliant and full and those who walked there while the waters of the fountains peaked and fell knew that Roman Catholicism had taken an enormously important turn. It would have been foolish then to think that the future was assured; experienced men feared the worst. As Karl Rahner said before the Vatican Council opened: "We are not ready; it is coming 50 years too soon."

The worst has not by any means arrived, but what has come to pass is not entirely good. Gustav Weigel once quipped in Rome: "All things human, given enough time, go badly." So with reform and renewal—and also with revolution—in the Church.

I recently visited a community of sisters prominent in the reform movement over the last few years. "Secularization" has taken effect. The results are not altogether pleasant. In the past, sisters have by and large been among the most interesting women one encountered: dedicated and single-minded, but also complicated and struggling. Whatever their social and educational level (poor, lower-middle class, or well-attuned college graduates), they by and large developed a richer and more disciplined inner life than their sisters and former associates who remained "in the world."

In this community subtle changes had clearly occurred. A

profound emotional struggle still goes on, but it appears to be one of confusion, uncertainty, wavering purpose, a sliding between several opposing sets of ideals and ways of life. Perhaps these are only growing pains or transitional symptoms. But a certain fruitful tension seems to have slipped out of the bow: all sense of transcendence. One no longer senses those "vibrations" which arise from a life of prayer, or from persons living in the presence of God. One finds oneself among women, now not so willingly unmarried, whose conversation and sentiments have become conventional to liberal persons of their age, sex, and occupation. One hears views that are uncritically and enthusiastically liberal (or radical). It is as if there were no deep roots, only a shift in peer-group ideals. (Occasionally one meets a former sister who *has* the deep roots, and still has the sense of prayer; and the contrast is striking.)

One senses the absence of the life of prayer everywhere in middle-aged groups: married persons, priests, activists of all sorts. Even among conservatives, complaints about the Catholic revolution do not concern the life of the spirit (except as a cover for other interests). They concern uniformity, obedience, good manners, the solemn mystery of the old liturgy.

Conventional liberal wisdom reigns. It counts today as a good reason for leaving the priesthood that one is in love with a woman. Who would believe a priest who said he was leaving because he had lost his faith? Probably not even his bishop. For to speak of faith is not to speak credibly or convincingly. Faith is not taken to be serious or real; sex is. Both the man involved and his acquaintances will heed the imperative *cherchez la femme* in order to "explain" his action in terms of the prevailing sense of reality.

On the other hand, what do conservatives—what do bishops—mean when they appeal to faith? They seem to mean a resolve

20

of will duty-bound to feel or at least to speak about things in a special way, in a special language, structuring all their perceptions accordingly. Or else they seem to mean an undisturbed, unquestioned, simple way of life—as when they point to phenomena they observed on their last trip to Ireland (but not to Italy?). In either case, they do not seem to mean that critical, gentle, unwavering sense of living in the burning light of conscience, undeceived by fraudulence, seeing matters even in the Church as they are and calling them by their names—as, for example, Flannery O'Connor did. There is a difference between faith as a set of blinders and faith as a set of eye-openers; and the test lies in the accuracy of concrete perception and the honesty of concrete speech.

It is sad to see so many good spirits, on whom hopes for reform, renewal, and revolution heavily depend, exchanging one form of faith (surely one they had more deeply appropriated) for another (which they wear uncomfortably)—a liberal Catholic one for a just plain liberal one (often now, of course, a radical one).

What is it to be a Catholic today? I am not at all certain that I know the answer. I know that it is to belong to an historical people, a complicated and diverse people, who have thought, felt, and lived in many different cultural forms in a long and often ugly history. History, Hegel said, is a butcher's bench: surely never more than in the liberal era. I am unable to find any set of phrases or conceptions or life-forms which at all times and at all places defined what it is to be a Catholic. I conclude that they are Catholic who think of themselves as Catholic, and who shape their lives (in quite personally and culturally distinct ways) around reflection on the Word, the celebration of the eucharist, and a universal sense of peoplehood. The centralized structure around Pope and Curia, and the use of Rome as a symbol for universal peoplehood, now seem inadequately Catholic, neither true enough nor human enough nor close enough to the Gospels.

Many years ago, despite my great respect for them as men and as Catholics, I regarded Charles Davis as one who had constructed a model of a liturgical Church, and Gregory Baum as one who had constructed a model of a scriptural Church, both models being too widely separated from the church of daily experience. Catholic faith is more adequately placed in a people, with all the faults—personal, social, cultural, and institutional—of peoples. A people is an historical, ordinary, diffuse, various complex, knit by blood and habit and striving and concrete experiences; neither ideal nor noble nor especially spiritual, but flesh and blood. Still, in the Catholic people are memories, sentiments, images that are so much a part of the texture of my being —not only by birth but also by choice and long self-tutoring— that I think I could not erase them now if I tried.

Were I a priest, I am not certain that I would have been able to endure the double jeopardy in which priests now must place themselves: to be part of the people *and* part of the present concrete institution. Since I removed myself from that second jeopardy, how can I not share sympathetically in a similar choice made by others? And yet my deepest feelings of regard and favor go out to those who, knowing what I knew, felt themselves temperamentally strong enough to undergo that second painful struggle. If the present political form of Catholicism is ever to be cast out of our common Catholic experience as an unnecessary and a cruel abomination, many will have to throw it over from *within*.

The Church is not a spiritual, non-institutional body or a movement; a people must have institutional structures if it is to endure, to make corporate decisions, and to carry along the cultural riches of the past. The people's cultures of other times,

22

other places, are no less rich for our reflection today than black culture or the newly discovered cultures of the poor. Institutional structures are instruments, not ends, and they are subject to the sociological laws of routinization, bureaucracy, and officialdom. By definition, neither truth nor honesty nor justice nor community are their latent—though they are certainly their proclaimed —aims. Self-preservation is uppermost. The Roman Catholic institution has been flexible under previous conditions of cultural crisis; the will to endure is stronger than any single institutional form. The people outlive the forms. The task of the Catholic people today is to throw off the institutional weight that has too long afflicted them. The institution belongs to them, not they to it.

One expects officials to defend by all means necessary their own importance, function, centrality, indispensability; to proclaim themselves accordingly; to condemn opposing views as heretical; to insist on loyalty oaths to the central bureaucracy, both regarding its doctrines and regarding its practices. What else would vested interests in a rich bureaucracy do?

There are two inaccurate views of the matter to be equally avoided. The first is that "the people" have some sort of existence apart from their institutions. The second is that "the people" are indistinguishable from their institutions. The forms of institutions come and go; the people remain. For three centuries there were no church buildings; for centuries no cardinals; for centuries no prince-bishops; for centuries no daily and self-consciously world-governing popes; for centuries no curia in touch with the whole world by television, radio, and air mail service. Faith need not reside in an institution-less people; nor in an apology for the present institutional forms.

Yet it would be a further mistake to imagine that institutional change comes by being preoccupied with institutional change.

23

The present structure of Roman Catholicism must be altered, in a virtually total way. But our best prospect for altering it is first of all to steep ourselves in the resources of spirit accessible to our people—to find in them (in the Spirit among them) the instincts and courage required. It is, secondly, indispensable to think concretely and administratively, wisely and structurally, about what shape to give our institutions so that they will be healthier and sounder three generations hence. There is no possibility of doing away with institutional forms.

It is the first task which thinkers in the last few years have too much neglected, often because they so took it for granted, or had so many blows to strike (while the iron was hot) in the second task. Catholicism is above all else the presence of God, a growing more profound and skillful in exploring the trackless regions of solitude and despair; it is a joy which comes from tasting unmistakable but ambiguous reality; a refusal to flinch from personal life as it is; a sense of peoplehood (which is not the same as community feeling); a vivid appetite for thick steaks, good cigars, and beautiful men and women; a possibly unverbalized conviction that life is unfair and that freedom is never entirely won, and a eucharistic meal in which all these themes and others (each Catholic celebrates his own constellation) are gathered up.

The eucharist, however, cannot be celebrated unambiguously today. A great deal about it is false—on the one hand, the institutional structure it at present represents; on the other, the widespread romantic and anarchic contempt for structures (now almost as prevalent as ersatz community). Hence, even the eucharist itself functions for us as a criterion of the honesty, solitude, and peoplehood yet to be built up, in exactly the same way as marital intercourse sets a standard for married persons which they do not meet. We are a wayfaring people, set upon by the

24

self-interested "altruism" of bureaucrats and by our own weaknesses.

For all that, God through our occasionally accurate perception, critical love, self-scouring honesty, and slow, single steps toward self-liberation makes his presence known to us. Through such uniquely personal and communal activities, men participate in his life. All men may recognize themselves as one universal people; yet some are linked, besides, to the deeds and events of Catholic Christian history. It is a sense of participation in a life divine as well as human of which one most senses the lack among liberal and radical Catholics today, not to mention among equivalent Protestants. These days, do only atheists and young persons know the silence of contemplation?

2

Honesty and Freedom

THERE are not, Pascal wrote, three honest men in a century. He did not mean there were two or one. He meant that you cannot trust anyone over thirty, or anyone under thirty, and least of all yourself. Few personal achievements are more ambiguous and evanescent than honesty; few concepts are trickier. That honesty is possible we know, not directly, but indirectly: Unless it were sometimes possible there would be no such behavior as dishonesty. Of dishonesty we have ample experience, and for its presence in others we have quite sharp noses. To see how prevalent dishonesty is, it is convenient to observe the behavior of those whose profession is said to be truth or intellectual honesty. Professors, even of religion or philosophy or science, are rather easily flattered. They commonly overestimate their own importance in the world and in the history of ideas, and they often so badly misunderstand their intellectual opponents that one cannot attribute the failure merely to lack of acumen. The rudder of honesty, in brief, is deflected by many currents.

In order to understand the relation of honesty to intellectual life, particularly as it bears upon religious men, it is helpful to establish several interrelated perspectives. My discussion attempts to single out four such perspectives and to describe them clearly: the genetic, the dialectical, the universal, and the concrete. The reader may find, however, that he will wish to call the perspectives by different names, or to describe them somewhat differently. All the better, for the effort is one in which both writer and reader have a powerful stake. I do not wish to paper over the issues with words; I would hope the reader might recognize the relevant experiences in his own life. The test to be met by the work of this chapter, then, lies in the living experience of the reader. We are not playing games with words, but attempting together to illuminate our human experience.

The Genetic Perspective

Words are tools, means and not ends, poor instruments at best for articulating our experiences and insights. They express the subtleties of our emotions clumsily, and the nuances of our relations to one another and to our environment hardly at all. Ask a class of college students, "What color is the sky today?" and they will answer, "Blue. What do you mean what color is the sky? It's blue." We have a very limited series of words to name colors: azure, cobalt, blue. But at any one moment the eye can discern dozens of variations in the sky. We settle for rough approximations and often even gross inaccuracies; yet usually our ordinary language works quite well. Still, it tends to blunt our perceptions, to blind and to mislead us, and to impoverish our awareness. For words stimulate and direct and shape attention, they do not merely express it. Some words are dead and others live; some open our eyes, while others merely busy them. We are in the debt of poets who can jab worn words for us and awaken them from their pragmatic slumbers.

One of the sources of dissatisfaction with contemporary writing in ethics in England and America is that too many philosophers take language out of its personal matrix, without attention to the experience, the perception, and the insight that ethical words embody. The same word—"love," for example, or "moral"—used at different stages of one's life has a different meaning. "Honestly" has one meaning on the lips of a campaigning politician or a television adman, and another on the lips of a young man going to jail for his convictions. "Free world" means something worth dying for to some, and diplomatic duplicity to others.

"Honesty," in particular, is a word whose meaning is deepened by the experience of life. (All moral words seem to have this characteristic; when we use them we express in some way not only our emotions, our cognitions, or our convictions but also the texture of our lived experience.) "Honesty" is not a word that lies flat, in a nonhistorical, merely logical and univocal frame of reference. The way one uses the word depends upon one's own moral, intellectual, social, and even political development. To explore the meaning of the word "honesty" is to explore, in a manner demanded by other ethical words as well, the resources of one's own experiences of life. The mere study of the logic of ethical words, without attention to the living connections of these words with the experience of historical persons, is a fraud. It may be an interesting game, but it is not ethics and it does not illuminate action.

No word, perhaps, is more important ethically to young people today than "honesty." It represents a value that almost every student is likely to rank at the very top of his scale of ethical values. One college student recently examined in a paper how his understanding of the human experiences pointed to by the word had changed over the years. As a child, he had thought of honesty as "telling the truth," that is, as asserting in conventional speech a description of events or thoughts or actions that coincided with what he took to be the case concerning those events, thoughts, actions. In school, the word came to be associated with obeying the rules regarding homework and tests: doing his own work, not cribbing or copying the work of others. Gradually, "honesty"

28

came to mean "authenticity": coming to his own decisions (as distinguished from what authority figures or peers wanted him to do) and sticking to them. He found the notion of honesty getting trickier by the month: How could he be *sure* his decisions were his own?

Later, this student's conception of honesty began to shift from a focus on autonomy to a focus on relations with others: He wished to be "honest" in his hates and his loves, his resentments and his joys. So highly did he value honesty that it now came to be, it seemed, his sole ethical value. He was in love with a girl and, so long as they were "honest" with one another, he thought it appropriate to sleep with her. His honesty became suspect in his own eyes, however, when he began to notice that he did not, in fact, tell her all of his feelings about their relationship. Sometimes he resented her, or was bored by her; he did not wish to make love at some of the moments she did, even when he cooperated. Sometimes he felt a strong love for her, at other times not, but in speech and action he tended to express the love and to be silent about the indifference. He was not sure whether he should express every vagrant sentiment he felt. On some occasions, frankness seemed destructive and he suspected it may even have been, on his part, malicious (he found it hard to discern his own motives). At different points in time, he evaluated his own actions differently, sometimes thinking his conscious motives valid, at other times suspecting more unpleasant latent meanings within them. "Honest, yes," he wrote, "but honest to *what*? Which part of me is myself? If I try to express every sentiment I discover floating through my head, the outcome will be almost total self-preoccupation. Besides, the sentiments are self-contradictory and change constantly."

In particular, the young man decided that honesty (whatever it entailed) was not the only criterion for helping him judge his

29

relationship with his lover. He got to thinking about honest sadists, honest bigots, honest Nazis. But, most of all, the ambiguities involved in honesty itself captured his attention. His chain of reasoning led him (without his having read Sartre) in the direction of Sartre's analysis of *mauvaise foi:*[1] The moment that he thought he had a *self* to be honest to, that self was passing to another and different moment. In this perception, honesty seems to be an impossible achievement, and anyone who claims to be honest or sincere is a liar. We must, he concluded, accept honesty as a regulative ideal in whose light we detect manifold and obvious forms of dishonesty, without being able to accept it unequivocally as a characteristic of any of our own actions.

The point of this extended example is that honesty as a moral ideal involves the one who pursues it in a voyage through many levels, types, and densities of experience. Its demands are not simple and direct, but complex and often quite ambivalent. Just as Socrates saw growth in wisdom as a more thorough recognition of his own ignorance, so also growth in honesty seems to imply a more complicated recognition of the polymorphousness of one's own consciousness. At different times one tends to have different perceptions of events, self, and others. The example seems to show, then, that the metaphor for the investigation of ethical terms like "honesty" should be that of a voyage, a journey, a pilgrimage involving new and different and more complicated discoveries. The metaphor of a "language game," with its suggestion of well-defined checkers moved about in patterns on a single plane, is lamentably inadequate as a model for ethical experience, and hence for ethical speech. Even the metaphor of a drama, with its script, its players, its roles, and its moves, does injustice to the surprises, spontaneities, and unfamiliar perplexi-

---

[1] Jean-Paul Sartre, *Being and Nothingness,* New York, 1966, pp. 56 ff.

ties that characterize ethical experience. To understand the meaning of honesty, as an experience and as a notion, requires the employment of a genetic perspective. It is a relevant question to ask the moralist, "At what stage of the journey do you begin your discussion? How simple-minded do you ask your listener to be? How far can you carry us in interpreting our complex experience?"

The Dialectical Perspective

The implication of the genetic perspective is that one can grow in honesty; hence, that decline or corruption are also possible But what shall we use as the measure of growth or decline? Men appear, in fact, to choose different measures. They seem to be *free* to choose their own measure. Hence, the philosopher is tempted to move the discussion to a second level and to focus his attention upon the characteristics of that freedom. Freedom in this sense is the capacity to choose one's own measure, goals, frame of reference, methods of proceeding, patterns of perception, image of oneself, and the like; in a word, the capacity to shape one's own "horizon."[2] No doubt, the child inherits the structuring of his horizon from his parents and from the culture in which he lives. But our American culture, in particular, is highly pluralistic and complex and full of inner conflict. To a large extent, then, the child, the adolescent, and the young man find themselves called upon to choose among alternative horizons. They are pulled this way and that, and their own complex impulses incline them in alternative directions. Every single decision they make is conditioned by a great many factors; there is no such thing as an unconditioned choice. Still, they

[2] See my *Belief and Unbelief*, New York, 1965, pp. 57–58.

themselves must choose to reinforce this line of conditioning or that, to put themselves in the way of these experiences or those, to select this line of inquiry or that. Not to choose is also a choice. Choice is impossible to avoid.

During the early years in one's life an enormous number of decisions are made over which one has no control: time and place of birth, methods of child rearing, actions and attitudes of parents, social position, cultural context, early schooling, etc. Consequently, the power to criticize the inherited horizon and to take responsibility for reshaping it is a difficult achievement. One begins in a kind of helplessness and heteronomy. Only slowly, step by painful step, does one achieve one's own, always incomplete, liberation. Once again, the illuminating metaphor is that of a voyage.

Honesty and freedom appear to point to complementary aspects of the same voyage. Honesty is the component of intelligence, the light, the self-anchored fidelity by which one proceeds. The exercise of freedom is the component of desire and determination, the resolution, the courage, by which one takes responsibility upon oneself. Honesty without freedom is idle; freedom without honesty is blind.

Thus, to speak about growth in honesty is also to speak about growth in freedom, and vice versa. Unless one has courage, one will not be able to face the truth about one's own conditioning and inclinations. Unless one has honesty, one will not be able to see the source or the import of one's actions. In a great many of our actions, we play out parts in dramas we did not invent, or would not consciously admit to choosing, or imagine to be more liberating than they are. A professor imagines himself to be cool, objective, open-minded, reasonable, and acts out his part, within the horizon permitted by his image of the expert, the reasonable man, the scientist. Within that horizon, his conduct may be flawless. The limitations of that horizon, however, may cripple his humanity.

Consequently, a discussion of honesty must take into account the interplay between freedom and honesty, and the different levels of self-awareness and self-liberation that men attain. No man lives within an infinite horizon, such that he always sees other persons and himself accurately; on the contrary, each man struggles in the toils of his own limited self-awareness and self-liberation. His dishonesties and unfreedom make it improbable that he will perceive other persons or their positions accurately. More often than not, he will force others and their positions through the distorting screens of his own perceptions, hacking them down to those perceptions. When he accuses others of dishonesty, he is often sketching a portrait of himself. A philosopher who writes a history of philosophy or lectures on the work of some other man reveals his own depth and sensitivities. (And the one who, recognizing this, lectures on others in order to show off his own talent is not a lover of wisdom.)

In a word, we must not be misled by pretenses to "objectivity." Those who lecture on ethics have themselves a personal ethical history. The degree of their self-awareness and self-liberation affects their perception of ethical experience and ethical discourse. Those who imagine themselves to be objective merely reveal their insensitivity to the role of self-awareness and self-liberation in ethical perception. They speak without knowing what they say.

Let us summarize the first two perspectives: Honesty must be understood in a genetic perspective; we grow in honesty, or decline; we are not born honest, but struggle to become so, extending our self-awareness over an ever-wider circle of our lives. Secondly, honesty and freedom are complementarily related in our growth toward a fuller humanity, as also in our corruption and decline. The measure of growth and decline is the degree to which a man becomes aware of the determinants of his own consciousness and behavior and takes responsibility for shaping them. To choose some other measure than honesty and freedom is to take responsibility for a choice; and not to be aware of what one is doing, or why, is to heighten the probabilities of self-deception and unfree choice. The demands of honesty and freedom are so strong that they generate the need for rationalizations to cover our flights from honesty and our escapes from freedom. Man is a rationalizing, freedom-fearing animal, who is only sometimes honest and free.

The Universal Perspective

Men are sometimes honest and, within limits, free. Conversions occur; genuine breakthroughs in personal insight or freedom are achieved. Moreover, if not all at once at least one by one, rationalizations are detected and escapes from freedom duly pointed out. Consequently, the presence in us of capacities for honesty and freedom, struggling to be more fully developed, is unmistakable. Perhaps no other dynamic is so quietly, insistently evident in the betrayals and tragedies that mark our history. Human beings wish to be honest and free and even small evidences of honesty and freedom pierce to the heart. Men do not boast of being dishonest or unfree; even the most malicious cover their deeds with coveted names.

I have argued in other places[3] that the religious quest is identical with the voyage toward honesty and freedom. The point of such an assertion is not that every honest and free man is, by definition, religious. It is rather that religion offers an *interpre-*

[3] See my *Belief and Unbelief* and also *The Experience of Nothingness,* New York, 1970.

tation of the fact that honesty and freedom sometimes occur. The experience of those who are free and honest, but not religious, contributes (in the eyes of the religious man) to that interpretation. The atheist, of course, rejects the religious interpretation, even though his honesty and freedom provide some of the facts which that interpretation is meant to illuminate. His reasons for rejecting the religious interpretation are many and powerful; in any case, the argument between the theist and the atheist is not our concern here. I wish instead to set forth the connection, as I see it, between the experience of honesty and freedom and belief in God.

No one sees God; God (if there is a God) is hidden. Moreover, the experience of God is not direct; it is always mediated—mediated at the very least by our own sense organs, imaginations, intelligence. In both Jewish and Christian traditions, Aristotle's image resonates—man stands before God as the owl before the sun. God exceeds our capacities for understanding. The consequence of these two facts—the hiddenness of God and the disproportion between God and man—is that man knows God only indirectly, by metaphor, by analogy, by extrapolation from human experience.

There are two reasons why the human experiences of honesty and freedom furnish us with the most accurate basis available for speaking of the Jewish and Christian God. First, if we do not take honesty and freedom as the base of our analogies, then God tends to be conceived in a way that disregards or minimizes men's honesty and freedom; our relations to him becomes heteronomous, and the true God becomes indistinguishable from Baal or other tyrannical gods. Second, the fact that men are sometimes honest and sometimes free, in a world of so much dishonesty and so much slavery, is what prompts us to speak of God. Human evolution is a struggle for honesty and freedom (the building up of the kingdom). The surprising successes of honesty and freedom in history are sought also in our personal lives; the race itself and each member struggles for liberation. Moreover, a novelist who creates characters he himself does not manipulate, whose purposes and impulses elude his own designs, is greater by far than a novelist whose creatures are wooden. In such a view, men are free, God is not a puppeteer, and history has a point: the expansion of liberty.

To speak in that way, however, does not go far enough to represent the Christian and Jewish view. The fact that men are sometimes honest and sometimes free (and that they sometimes love one another) makes some men wonder about the riddle of our existence. For often we are content to think that the questions how and why and whence are unanswerable, and content to imagine ourselves as part of mechanical, causal chains of great complexity. But occasionally the taste of freedom is too sharp and the heroism required for honesty is too striking. We are led to wonder if the force of honesty within us, and the drive for freedom, are not a key that unlocks the riddle, a key revealing that God is the power of honesty, God is the power of freedom, and all of us participate—to the degree we choose—in his life. If one reads the Jewish and Christian scriptures in this light, it is plain that God is not a thing, object, or being "out there" and distant from us, but a force driving us, judging us, drawing us, from within. The chief manifestation of divine life in the universe is the human struggle for honesty and freedom.

I am not suggesting, as John Dewey[4] appears to, that we merely *call* our highest ideals God. I am suggesting that our highest activities (honesty, freedom, and—I will stress in chapter eleven—community) are our participations in a divine life that

[4] John Dewey, *A Common Faith*, New Haven, 1934.

manifests itself throughout our universe. For many persons today such an image of the world is alien, falsifying, and impossible to maintain. I do not wish, in this context, to defend it. I wish only to call attention to it. For persons who think that God's presence in man is identical with man's honesty, self-criticism, and taking up of responsibility, there is a certain simplification in the problem of existence. To maximize honesty and freedom is to live more thoroughly in God, and God in self. To be faithful to the drive to raise questions (faithful to wonder and inquiry) and faithful to self-determination is to be faithful to God. To obey God is not to obey taboos, ordinances, or doctrines but to obey conscience; and on the other hand, conscience is tutored by the experiences of argument, challenge, directive, warning, law, failure, success, and, in a word, by hard encounter with all those things that cannot be wished away. To be dishonest or unfree is to turn away from God (*aversio a Deo*), to sin against the light; it is not so much rebellion as self-mutilation. As it is difficult to be honest and free, so it is difficult to know when one is being faithful to God and when one's purported honesty is not merely a sophisticated betrayal. We work out our salvation in fear and trembling. There are not three persons faithful to God in a century.

Not only is the religious quest identical with the quest for honesty and freedom. It is also the most central and radical drive of the personality. Commonly, the religious orientation is more integrative, more pervasive, more comprehensive than political, social, marital, educational, or other orientations.[5] Moreover, as Luckmann, Berger, and O'Dea argue,[6] the word "religious" must

[5] See, e.g., Gordon W. Allport, *The Individual and His Religion,* New York, 1965, and Adrian van Kaam, *Religion and Personality,* Englewood Cliffs, N.J., 1964.

[6] Thomas Luckmann, *The Invisible Religion,* New York, 1967; Peter L.

be understood in a context broader than the context of limited historical institutions: denominations, sects, churches. The basic, central orientation by which a man symbolizes his sense of direction, his relations to the world and to others, and his meaningfulness (or meaninglessness): *That* is his religious view. Such an orientation is not merely philosophical (conceptual), for it is rich in latent and symbolic content, and it is acted out in rituals and institutions and expressions that are more like the framework of inquiry or language than like questions within the framework. The word "religious," however, makes too many persons uncomfortable; they feel that its use somehow traps them into enforced relations with an unwanted God. But the point is that whether or not there is a God, and whether there is question of theists or atheists, all men in fact act out their own personal symbols of meaning, relation, and ends; and these ultimate personal symbols are subject to analysis, comparison, and criticism. Theology, I will argue in chapter ten, has as its central task the study of such symbols.

Still, the most pressing problem in relating honesty to religion does not arise on this level of generality. In my view, the quest for honesty *is* the religious quest; I interpret the quest for honesty among us as an indication of man's participation in a life not merely his own, but divine. Perhaps a majority of philosophers, experiencing a similar drive for honesty, do *not* interpret it theistically. Each remains free to select the interpretation that seems to him most adequately to illuminate the labyrinth of human life (and free, also, to argue with others about opposed interpretations). There is no coercive procedure for determining the criteria for this selection. We argue with one

Berger, *The Sacred Canopy*, New York, 1967; Thomas F. O'Dea, *The Sociology of Religion*, Englewood Cliffs, N.J., 1966.

another about such criteria, about the selection of the interpretation, about the interpretations themselves, and about the facts we believe ourselves to be interpreting. I am content that such arguments go on ceaselessly; they are the genuinely interesting ones: Who are we, under these stars, with the breeze upon our faces?

The Concrete Perspective

The most pressing problem in relating honesty to religion, however, lies within the fourth of our perspectives; it has to do with the problem of belonging to a particular, concrete, institutionalized expression of religion—such as the Catholic. To belong to an institution is ipso facto to belong to a time-conditioned network of relations, a social structure, an organism in which roles, offices, and a conceptual system have already been formalized. Moreover, the Roman Catholic institution tends to sacralize these relations, structures, and formal expressions; the Vatican itself tends to endow their concrete historical form with a finality, absoluteness, and authority that stands against and contradicts the flow of history. I find the sacralizing and immobilizing tendencies among the Roman Catholic people destructive on human grounds and inadequate on Catholic grounds. They are in this epoch a perversion of the Roman Catholic principle, a perversion all the more deleterious when they are championed, as they often are, by popes, curial officials, bishops, and official documents. It is no surprise to me that those in authority should wish to sacralize that authority and to immobilize any efforts to humanize and to Christianize it. Their self-interest encourages the ideology they so strictly (and ably) defend. Nonetheless, they and their ideology must be displaced from the center of Roman Catholic life. Their usual tactic is to excommunicate reformers. But after four centuries of experiment, reformers have learned a variety of counter-tactics. One of these is neither to fear nor to honor excommunication. The reformer *is* a Catholic; that cannot, after all, be taken away, and by all the energies of persuasion at his command he may resolve to persuade his fellows to renew and to reform the institutions that serve his people.

Yet it is difficult to be honest in such a role. Why should one bother to remain a Catholic? Is there any hope that such an entrenched institution is reformable? And is it worth the effort to master the orthodoxy so well that one can turn it against itself as a weapon of reform (as Jesus himself did)? This is not the place to offer extended answers to such basic questions.[7] Suffice it to say that as a human being I owe my origin, my beginnings, and a great deal of my development to the sources of life still nourished in the Roman Catholic people; and I have learned an implicit respect for the necessity, power, and value of institutional forms. My objection to the present form of Roman Catholicism is not that it is an institution, but that it is the kind of institution it is. On the premises of Roman Catholicism itself, it does not have to be—it should not be—what it is.[8] Historical institutions, in general, are worth saving by reform when possible, by revolution when necessary; to construct new ones is infinitely more difficult and less promising of success. We are an historical race; we carry our history with us; I would not wish merely to escape it.

To remain a Roman Catholic, however, is a tricky business. I

[7] I have attempted to face these issues in many of my writings to this point. See especially *The Open Church*, New York, 1964; *A New Generation*, New York, 1964; and *A Time to Build*, New York, 1968.

[8] See, for example, Hans Küng, *The Church*, New York, 1968, and John McKenzie, S.J., *Authority in the Church*, New York, 1967. See also *A New Catechism*, New York, 1968.

have often found myself repeating inherited words I did not understand or, upon reflection, did not accept. I have often had to think out an issue in two ways, once in the historical context in which it originated and again in a contemporary context, and sometimes one effort suffers because of the other. But that tension, I believe, is a fruitful one. It inoculates me against some contemporary prejudices and against some traditional ones. It enriches my sense of complexity and ambiguity, my feeling for the unconceptualizable gaps between the points of view that separate persons, times, and cultures; such points of view can never be laid out so logically as to yield item-by-item comparison.

Yet it remains a moot question whether one can remain both Catholic and a contemporary man, with honesty. I am impressed by the lives of friends and literary figures who appear to be doing it, or to have done it. Honesty is also difficult for the man of the Enlightenment, the Jew, the follower of Karl Barth.

At two points, however, honesty is especially difficult for the Catholic. First, the Catholic believes two seemingly contradictory propositions: that in some privileged, extraordinary way God manifests his power (honesty and freedom) in the history of the Roman Catholic Church; and that the capacity of the structures and the members of that Church for betraying honesty and freedom are unlimited. The record of the Church in these matters is often dismaying. Thus the Catholic learns a kind of "double think": he learns to face evil squarely and frankly; on the other hand he learns to look for the underside of evil—the good that is unintentionally and indirectly but inevitably done by it. "*O felix culpa!*" Saint Augustine cried, praising the God who draws good even from malice. This form of double think can easily become a tool to justify anything. Consequently, the Catholic is in special danger of lending his support to a corrupt institution, when perhaps he should rather fight against it. The

41

proof of honesty lies in the efforts made to diagnose its ills precisely and to reform them effectively. The strides taken by the Catholic reform movement since 1962 have in this respect been heartening.

Second, the vastness of the intellectual critique which must be leveled against and within Catholicism provides, by its very amplitude, warm folds for the larvae of dishonesty.[9] In order to rethink large concepts like divinity, incarnation, papal authority, transubstantiation, virgin birth, original sin, and the like, in a way that brings their power of illumination to bear upon contemporary life, such a total mental revolution is required that no one man can achieve it alone and each man's personal progress is necessarily uneven. Consequently, Catholics commonly find their minds and sensibilities inhabited by contradictory and antithetical materials. It is relatively easy to ignore the contradictions or to take refuge in umbrella explanations like "demythologizing" and "hermeneutics" and "new theology." The task of translation from ancient Jewish and Christian cultures to the present staggers the critical faculties. There may be some continuity between the psychic universe of the fishermen who were the first apostles and that of the well-heeled priests and parishioners of the United States, who wheel their Oldsmobiles and Chryslers out of the parking lot after mass to hurry home for the Superbowl game on television. But that continuity would be extremely difficult to define.

Hence, even the most basic question of all is excruciatingly difficult to meet: "What does it mean to be a Catholic in the United States in the present generation? What ought one to believe? How ought one to shape one's sensibilities, imagination,

---

[9] See Daniel Callahan, *Honesty in the Church,* New York, 1965, for an analysis of many forms of Catholic dishonesty, especially among liberal Catholics.

and affectivity? What should one do?" The answers to these questions are not *given,* not to this or to any generation. They must be invented anew in every generation, out of meditation upon the basic texts and traditions of the Catholic people. These resources are rich, various, and liberating. It has been a Catholic tradition, for example, to borrow shamelessly from the best wisdom of the age and slowly to move toward assimilating it ultimately as "Catholic." Most of what we today know as Catholic was accumulated in that fashion. There is nothing wrong with being the first Catholic in your generation to perceive the best riches of the age and to mark them out for acquisition: to live out for the first time an untried style of life.

It will surely be objected by guardians of orthodoxy—particularly by those atheists[10] who challenge religious persons according to the orthodox statements and deeds of the past—that if one does not accept, literally and irrevocably, the creeds, symbols, and documents of one's church, then one is not a Christian (*a fortiori* not a Catholic) at all. The criterion for being a Christian today is not, in any case, easy to establish. It would be odd if, in order to be a Catholic, one had to think in first-century metaphors and thirteenth-century philosophy. It would be exceedingly odd if one were not to interpret the historical documents and deeds of one's people with an accurate historical consciousness, making due allowance for time, place, circumstance, and intellectual horizon. The same principles would seem to obtain in interpreting contemporary papal documents.[11] An intelligent man would not expect an Italian pope, whose life has

[10] I think particularly of the works of Walter Kaufmann and Sidney Hook, as well as footnotes in the essays of such analytic philosophers as J. N. Findlay and Antony Flew.
[11] See Garry Wills, *Politics and Catholic Freedom,* Chicago, 1964, for an enlightened discussion of the interpretation of papal documents.

been compassed by the extraordinary cultural horizon of the Vatican, to speak very adequately on the meaning and purpose of lovemaking in married life, for example. At the same time, one would expect pope and Vatican to insist upon their prerogatives and to be blind to their limitations. An honest Catholic would sometimes publicly oppose them, and at other times ignore them.

To be a Catholic is, for many conservative persons, to belong to an institution whose concepts, rules, dogmas, and offices have already been defined and remain only to be accepted whole. In my view it is rather to belong to an historical people, to whom that institutional structure belongs and who must seriously reform it. A serious Catholic, I would argue, takes every historical dogma or practice of his people seriously, hoping to learn why it was that persons in earlier times (or yet today) found them illuminating and helpful. Such historical materials are not absolutes, but data, data to be understood, to be sifted and weighed and compared with other data. A serious Catholic wishes to ignore none of them and, on the other hand, to account for each. Some—like the celebration of community—are easily assimilable even today; others—like belief in angels—illuminate the past but offer little help today. Some of the data are central; others come and go, peripherally; each datum receives a different degree of emphasis, a different freight of meaning, in different epochs and different cultures and even in different personal lives. For Cardinal Spellman, Charles de Gaulle, Brendan Behan, and John F. Kennedy, the pieces in the kaleidoscope fell in quite different constellations.

The threat of heresy hangs over the head of every intelligent Catholic; often his non-Catholic friends are the first to utter it: "But you're not really a Catholic then!" One must learn to live lightly with heresy. The Catholic faith is not a set of propositions to which one must subscribe; it is a way of life. The conceptual formulations achieved during its long past require meditation and living assimilation. But such assimilation, precisely in proportion as it is living, is likely to be inexpressible in the conceptual formulations of the past. For both language and human experience change. The promises of God, that he is always with his people, do not on that account weaken. One becomes accustomed to searching for his presence in unaccustomed places: wherever the current demands of honesty and freedom lead. One draws hope and sustenance from reading history: The Church of Rome (like the human race in general) marches through time burning live offerings at every corner, then canonizing the victims as saints and doctors at other corners down the line. Besides, those who are docile to the present institutional structures are clearly heterodox, and so the only way to orthodoxy today is by a kind of heresy. It is not an instant heresy, made merely by bringing an issue to a boil; but a patient, learned, reflective kind of heresy, faithful as best it can be to the sinuous ways of—dare one say?—the Spirit. The room for self-deception is more ample than the slim probabilities of honesty.

Finally, it is worth stressing that all men live more by symbols, rituals, and dramatic metaphors than by words, creeds, or propositions. Writers on ethics are uncannily wide of the mark when they attempt to illuminate human action by analyzing acts of speech into their logical relationships. For ethical actions are not like logical moves. It is not the case that theories come first, or that imperatives come first, and then men act. Rather, it seems that men act out basic metaphors, like actors without a written script, more or less instinctively; only gradually, by repetition and conflict, do they become aware of the parts they are playing and the directions in which their instincts are moving them. To change their role and to alter their directions, conceptual clarity is not sufficient. To yield to the need for clarity, indeed, is to favor but one of many instincts, and to play analyst of verbal puzzles is to play but one of many roles; neither suffices for living a human life.

Consequently, one of the tasks to which honesty invites philosophers and theologians of all persuasions is to uncover the basic metaphors of their own work, to examine the symbols they are trying to live out, both as professionals and as men. A Catholic lives not only by the symbols and metaphors of his people but also by new ones of his own discovery and invention. Other men also live by metaphor and symbol. Particularly prominent in the academic world today are the symbols of reasonableness, dispassionateness, non-metaphysical pragmatism, and the myth of the objective observer. About these I wish to speak further in chapter twelve. Meanwhile, our next task must be to examine the chief Catholic symbols.

There are not three of us in our century who see our own key symbols and metaphors as others see them.

3

All the Catholic People

To be both Catholic and sectarian is to live a contradiction. Catholicism is not a sect. Even to describe it as an "ism" is to miss the point. To be a Catholic is, contrary to common opinion (even, alas, among Catholics), neither to be enrolled as a member of an institution, with officers and laws, nor to subscribe to a set of doctrines. To be a Catholic is to belong to an historical people. It is to enter into a certain kinship with the Jews and to accompany on an uncertain journey those other historical peoples of destiny: Muslims, Hindus, Buddhists.

Catholics are a people apart. They are different, even, from other Christians. Yet, as their name implies, they have an instinctive drive, an impulse, a necessity to diversify themselves, to learn from other peoples, to absorb strange and new lessons, and to become a variegated world-people, able to interact peaceably with all historical cultures. The mission of the Catholic people is not monolithic. The people are dispersed in order to become many and, while becoming many, to find a way of remaining one. The Catholic people are intended to live out in advance the unity and diversity for which the whole human race gropes.

The landmines awaiting those who would write about the Catholic people today, of course, make angels fear to tread. I do not write this eagerly, but because others, who have richer tongues, are silent. Everywhere one sees disarray, confusion, division. Those who have become "secular" seem to have lost their savor. It is incredible that many have surrendered their own riches in favor of the standard emptiness, and have chosen this particular moment to love the world uncritically. On the other hand, those who have not changed at all seem pitiably forlorn. Two hundred million persons have died by violence in 60 years, yet every Sunday the living drive to service-station masses, and then hurry home to forget, to resume.

How can one write about a people that, given a Jeffersonian 18 years per generation, is more than 100 generations old? It is easier for those who write three volumes on the dogmas, or five volumes on the laws. But to describe a living people? One must count heavily on one's intuitions, write as a novelist would write, see what (God forgive me) a poet would see. Inevitably, it is not the people one presents, but one's own sense of the people. Inevitably, one speaks for one's self alone. And yet, I would hope to write for conservatives and liberals, radicals and anarchists. I would like to write a reconciling text. I would like many, from many perspectives, to recognize themselves in what I write.

The fundamental point—that Catholics are a people—is as familiar as high school religion classes. But we are in a position today to draw new implications and to wrest a new vision from it. We have never before been able to take as seriously what it means to belong to one historical people among other historical peoples.

What, then, is a people? A people is multiform and various in any one era, even in a relatively homogeneous sample. But when a people extends itself through time, and enters many different cultures, builds homes, temples, farms, and markets in many different environments and social strata, then variety explodes into a milky way. Rich folk and hungry folk, shopkeepers and thieves, the shiftless and the exuberant, the despairing and the tranquil are parts of its pilgrimage. Clare Booth Luce and Graham

Greene, Charles de Gaulle and Mario Savio, Daniel Berrigan and Evelyn Waugh, Sophia Loren and Cesar Chavez, each find their place; Simone Weil, Pascal, Richelieu, Chaucer, Alexander VI, and countless unknown washerwomen, beggars, lechers, cheats, crooks, bishops, politicians, bankers, farmers, and millworkers belong. What sense of values were held in common by all?

It is no doubt a mistake to look for "something in common," some inner essence. An *ism* might have an essence; but Catholicism is not an *ism,* it is a people. The point of the category "people" is that it allows one to use a logic of resemblances rather than a logic of essences. There are certain constellations of values, attitudes, perceptions, and expectations among the Catholic people, constellations which come into focus, shift, and interchange. There is no possible way of defining the spirit of all Catholics at all times and in all places. Rather, certain themes occur here; and there another set partially overlaps the first; and over there yet another comes into prominence, muting some themes from the first and emphasizing a voice heretofore unheard.

A people grows according to historical experience, grows differently in different localities, in different social classes, under different economic pressures and political conditions. Canonically, liturgically, even in the narrowmost of times, more than a score of languages coexisted with Latin among the Catholic people. A people like the Catholic people, even where officially it has tried to employ a single canonized language like Latin, has a multiplicity of understandings of key words like "saint," "love," "law," "peace," "kingdom of God on earth," "hope." Were each Catholic in the world to say in words what he thought such symbols actually mean in his own experience, each would speak in a unique tongue. On the other hand, Catholics meeting one another recognize a oneness—not merely a oneness of reference to Rome, but rather a oneness of shared memory, a oneness of participation. To seek one's identity as a Catholic is, in John Dunne's phrase, "to search for God in time and memory," and that time, that memory, that God is social.

We are a people first before we are individuals. It is not true that individuals are converted first, and then joined together to form a community. Rather, Jesus called a people, among whom names were named. The community lives in us before we become conscious of it. Even those who at some moment in their lives are "converted" and "join the Church" characteristically experience a self-discovery, a discovery of a bond that long lived in them before they became aware of it. "In the beginning was the Word, and all things that were made, were made in him." The Word lies expressed in the heart of humanity, and those who penetrate through to that heart find how profoundly they have been one with their brothers from the beginning.

"You would not seek God," Pascal wrote, "unless you had already found him in your heart." The search itself *is* our participation in God's life. Men who try to understand and try to love, men who are what Albert Camus called in his special, nonecumenical sense, "men of dialogue," already live in God and God in them. Thus the Catholic people have a strange, unsociological composition. A Catholic sees in many persons brothers and sisters, who would not call themselves Catholic. It is not "semantic imperialism" that leads him to want to say: "But you are one of us!" It is respect for the heart of the matter: "In the beginning was the Word, and in him and through him and by him were made all things that are made." Those who do not lie against the light, but allow it to grow in them, are illuminated by the Word. The Catholic people has its roots in the primordial Word, that Alpha and Omega, that starting place and ending place of all community.

Yet "between the times," while "abyss cries out to abyss," in the historical middle period between silences, the Word is fractured, finitized, made concrete, in flesh. Human flesh is not one. Human communities are not one. There are diverse peoples. Hence, in a second and less profound but concrete sense the Catholic people are separable from other peoples; they are a distinctive people; their horizon is their own. It is not a fixed horizon, however. It is a horizon-on-the-move. Springing however inadequately, from the Word, it tends toward the Word. The movement is a spiral, directional and yet circular, its beginning being its end and yet all of history enfleshed along the route.

The Catholic vision suggested here is, perhaps, neo-Platonic with a strong modern sense of history. It is an effort to express two simultaneous truths, that *semper eadem* ("always the same") is not an adequate characterization of the real, concrete, world of history; and yet that the beginning point and the ending point are in the Word who became flesh. Eternity and time: Gemini-tension of Catholic experience.

The classical Protestant experience, by contrast, is much more thoroughly modern: history, time, evolution, progress, an unfinished God who grows with the world, the "eternal now" regarded as an illusion of pagan mysticism. Something profoundly Catholic warns us that the Protestant experience, while far richer in its appreciation of the modern world than our own tradition, is too narrow, is too shallowly rooted in the ancient world, is too unguardedly Faustian. The Catholic task is to absorb the modern motif and make it lie down together with some of the wisdom, not only of the Ancient West but also of the East. Catholic constellations of values include memory, present, and future, not one of these alone. A Catholic may well choose to exercise his wider possibilities by criticizing the Germanic cult of the future so prominent and so destructive today.

There is also a profound difference between being a Catholic and being a fundamentalist Protestant. The classical Protestant tries to learn from "the cultured despisers of religion" (Schleiermacher) and uses the modern world view as a criterion for the modern interpretation of Christianity. The fundamentalist Protestant resists the modern world view, in religious matters at least, and places his trust in the encounter between the preached word and the individual hearer.

Catholics, of course, often choose between similar options, between humanism and supernaturalism. But there is a strong intellectualist Catholic value which trusts ancient and medieval world views as well as the modern world view, and refuses to take any such standpoint as definitive. Its affection for the ancient and medieval standpoint arms it against the bias of the times, and gives it, if it does not merely retreat into traditionalism, a psychologically effective cultural relativism. (Many who claim to be cultural relativists have no mental leverage against the prejudices of the present.)

This Catholic possibility is grounded in a deep commitment to a whole, long historical past, a past full of contrasting viewpoints and opposing standards of perception and judgment. It is grounded in a fidelity to the vast range of historical experiences of all the Catholic people. Its assumption is that men in the past were not more stupid, less wise, and less in love with God than we.

What is it, then, to be a Catholic? The complex of standpoints, attitudes, drives, emotions and convictions can hardly be put into words, and certainly not in definitions. A "horizon"—that peculiar juncture of the subject and the range of all that he can see and do—cannot be stated. It can only be built up, sketched, symbolized, hinted at by indirection. To recreate it, many varied descriptions would be required. To enter into it, a conversion of life is required. Unless one lives in a certain way, some words do not make sense; or, often, one takes from them a meaning different from the one intended. Without becoming a Catholic, a sensitive man can "feel" himself into the position, checking his progress with friends and critics. But Catholics themselves must "feel" their way into their own identity as well.

For one's identity as a Catholic is not ready-made. Each man is different from every other (not in fact, for dreadful sameness is everywhere, but in possibility) and the Catholic people are served only when each man becomes a different kind of Catholic from every other. Duplication foreshortens Catholicity. Infinite variety is required.

One cannot, even, "discover" one's identity as a Catholic. One must invent it. To try to discover it would be to imagine (a) that it has been prearranged; and (b) that responsibility is a matter of conforming to some mysterious order. In fact, man is like God a creator; and his chief responsibility is to declare his own identity, to enunciate his own unique word, to utter a life that is not that of anyone else. To become an identifiable, unique word is to give fresh, finite, historical expression to that infinite Word, in whose image we are each uniquely made; to give him a finite face, a finite body, and finite agency in a new location in history. It is, at one and the same time, to be both uniquely ourselves and most freshly inhabited by him.

To be a Catholic is to be a member of a people. Each of these people live in Christ and he in them. A rather moving exchange occurs when we discover that the stranger to whom we speak is a Catholic. Not only sociology is at stake. Something courses in the blood: a common nourishing mystery participated in, a common memory of things past, sometimes a common unloosing of tongues and secret sentiments, sometimes a sharing in common inhibitions and blockages.

4

Picking and Choosing

To be a Catholic is to be a member of a people.

One objection to such a view takes the following form. If the Catholic people are diverse and various, and if there is no essence which all Catholics have in common, then individual Catholics are merely eclectic. Aren't we left with an arbitrary picking and choosing?

The question invites empirical observation. The God preached by Father X is not the God described by Father Y. Even though both ladies share the same age and background, the Christian insights of Sally Jones do not compare to those witnessed by Betty Button. Robert's temperament leads him to despise St. Aloysius and rather to admire the early Augustine; Alfred's character is so severe he "demythologizes" all the passages about Jesus and little children, Jesus in tears, and Jesus intimate with John.

Catholics, particularly those brought up within the narrow conventions of American Catholicism, are frequently misled by a recent abnormal emphasis on uniformity. That Catholics say the same words in a common creed does *not* mean that, experientially, intellectually or emotionally, those words have the same meaning for each of them. Notional assent is not real assent. Standing in rank is not the same as being converted inwardly.

If you ask an American Catholic, "What do you believe about X (contraception, say, or the virgin birth)?" he is likely to look at the floor for a moment, or at a far corner of the room. You know what he is doing. He is waiting for the words which he learned from his mother, pastor, sister, and catechism to click through the computer of his memory. When the pre-selected holes have been punched, his eyes light up and he says: "The Church teaches . . ."

"But I didn't ask you what the Church teaches," you halt him. "I asked you what *you* believe."

Then the American Catholic winces. He is unsure whether he can trust you to understand what he thinks about X. He is also unsure whether he can trust himself to face what he thinks about X.

The history of the Catholic people is long, and its doctrinal possibilities are as vast as the number of persons who have lived its doctrines. For it is not *saying* doctrines, orally or mentally, that constitutes genuine faith. It is rather the other way around. Life comes before doctrines. One changes one's way of living, and then the verbal expressions of doctrine may become intelligible. The modern "crisis of credibility" arises in lives to which other doctrines, but not those of the Catholic people, are "relevant." Pastors and parents have too often asked only that children get the words right; Catholic living, both conservative and liberal, has been allowed to become bright and modern and out of touch. The "crisis of faith" has been a crisis of culture, that is, a crisis of living. Only secondarily has it been a crisis of theological understanding. The inner power of "meaning" (which constitutes a culture) is lived before it is thematized.

This issue has been confused by too much talk in recent years about "conservatives" and "liberals," and by a failure to observe the distinction between "neighbor culture," "book culture," and "television culture."

A lawyer or real estate broker or gas-station attendant whose

Catholic style would be described as "conservative" is as likely as the next man to drive a shiny new car, to link the word "economics" very closely to words like "reality" and "hard truth," and to accept most of the psychic structures of American myths like competition, individualism, repressed sexuality, hard work, cleanliness. Such psychic structures are in conflict with others cherished among the Catholic people. In brief, "conservatives" are not necessarily out of date or irrelevant; often they are astonishingly modern, conformist, and willing to empty out their Catholic spirit for the sake of some patriotic substitute.

Similarly, liberals have often been misidentified. Characteristically, those who are called "liberal Catholics" are merely those who read theological books. There are, to be sure, conservative Catholic intellectuals; but, by and large, in the United States, book-minded conservatives do not think very highly of general American culture—and do not even like to use the good word "conservative" to describe it. For the average conservative Catholic takes his spiritual signals, not from books, but from his neighbors: their dress, aspirations, speech, emotions. The famous "liberal-conservative" debate has, in fact, often been a debate between "neighbor culture" and "book culture."

Liberal Catholics have tended to feed their faith by the latest books and articles, moving forward in sophistication and enthusiasm, as it were, by installments. Now, however, the "television culture" of the young has established new lines of sentiment, psychic energy, image, and perception. Television culture creates a new "movement." The cultural power of both neighbor culture and book culture is emptier for those who receive their cultural signals from a tribe dispersed everywhere but connected by electronic tubes. Basic metaphors for person, community, and other central notions of the Catholic people are now newly derived. The rapid movement of percepts sliding effortlessly through time (in the cinema and on television) weakens analytic intelligence, firm judgment and long-term decision. That is "meaningful" which is emotional, close, and warm. "Community" means kitten feelings, purry and gentle and innocent. "Person" means non-judgmental and affective openness.

There is no choice for a Catholic except to pick and choose. He must choose both which doctrines and symbols will shape his identity, and which cultural context he will connect himself to: neighbors, books, electronics.

He will do so unconsciously, if he does not do so consciously. He will do so for three reasons. The traditions of the Catholic people are far too rich; one finite man cannot possibly absorb all of them. Secondly, to absorb even some of the traditions of the Catholic people requires a lifetime; one must proceed step by step, in a process that is never fully accomplished. Thirdly, the traditions of the Catholic people do not come to a man complete, as a finished work merely to be accepted, but as a dynamism of hunches, orientations, perspectives, attitudes, inclinations, intuitions, convictions, and readiness (in the concrete present) to be freshly sensitive and intelligent. Such traditions are intended to prepare men to deal intelligently with the new, unparalleled present, and to anticipate the future. They require originality and intelligence: which is to say: selectivity.

In general, then, a fully generous attitude of loyalty to the Catholic people has two propelling forces: an all-embracing intention and a gradual appropriation. First, a man intentionally fixes his serious concern on *all* the data of the Catholic traditions. Whatever Catholics have believed, felt, thought, experienced he regards as part of his own patrimony, to be investigated and appropriated according to his lights, over a lifetime. Secondly, a generous and loyal Catholic begins by absorbing step by step into his actual living processes—experience, imagination, understanding, evaluating, deciding—those Catholic traditions, doctrines, symbols which in his view have the highest priority at the moment. Each creates his own distinctive identity.

Thus, a man may try to plumb first the mysteries of the trinity, incarnation, and eucharist—and leave for later his consideration of the assumption, papal infallibility, and the like. One cannot do everything at once. And one's relation to doctrine is not that of mere verbal assent, but of living practice. How can one live a doctrine whose point one does not understand, whose formulation is archaic and remote? Time, study, and sensitivity are required. Meanwhile, more urgent matters of the present—war and peace, riot and discontent, community polarization and hostility—may take doctrinal precedence.

As an example, a man who takes as the first reality of his life the building of community between distinct persons has grasped the point of the symbol of the trinity in human affairs. He makes man in the image of God. He has a realistic understanding of human life, and a powerful doctrinal position. He who merely repeats ancient words and concepts about the trinity is not living a doctrine but merely mummifying it.

That on this absurd, bloody, and fratricidal planet, community between persons is the "really real," the fundamental reality, the one reality on which to focus our attention, our energy, and our hopes, is an act of faith in what the doctrine of the trinity intends. The life of God is what is most real, and in human experience what is most like the unfathomable life of God is the communal life of distinct and separate persons who are one.

Beside the power of this mystery, talk of ecclesiastical politics (synods, curias, cardinals, legates) pales. What counts is the symbolic power of trinity, expressed today in building—despite the general madness—respect for one another among factious men.

No Catholic today, not even the pope, has absorbed all the doctrines, beliefs, wisdom, traditions, instincts, of the Catholic people. Each Catholic, consciously or unconsciously, has worked out his own personal selection. No one Catholic is a model for all the others. Each over the years has been picking and choosing, by drift or by choice, those living, appropriated symbols and doctrines that now shape his behavior. We criticize one another in the light of that infinite constellation of values which no one of us singly represents: the infinite riches of God's life, which are given us as a norm ("Be ye perfect"). Those riches are mirrored in the ceaseless series of men and women among the Catholic people down through history. It is as a community, a people, that we mirror back God's image.

Thus, it is astonishingly un-Catholic to fear diversity. It is the glory of the Catholic people, not that they are uniform, but that they are various. Only in variety can God's infinite life be represented by finite men, and God's people form a community to refract his image. The notion that by reciting the same words, by obeying the same canon laws, and by speaking the same Latin tongue, one can bring about unity of life distorts both the laws of the interior life of the individual psyche, and the laws of the social organism. Even the notion that uniformity and unity of doctrine ("*semper eadem*") are *attractive* is, on the face of it, implausible, shocking, and insupportable.

But what, then, establishes the unity of the Catholic people? What makes them one people? Those are Catholic people who decide to work out their lives by belonging to the Catholic people. They intend to shape their sensibilities, emotions, sensitivities, imaginations, judgments, and decisions according to trajectories and models operative among the Catholic people. To be a Catholic is to *intend* to belong to a people; to define one's identity thereby. But such an identity is not a finished one. Using the material of the past, and alert to new and heretofore unnoticed possibilities, Catholics can invent (do invent, even unthinkingly) a new present. They thus enrich, or impoverish, their people as former generations have. The Catholic people should not be, when each generation has run its course, what it was when that generation entered life. Moreover, each generation re-creates the whole people in its own fashion: lives out its own life, death, and resurrection. Each generation is both continuous with others and required to start afresh.

To be a Catholic is to be a member of a people. The life of the people is prior to symbols, creeds, doctrines, and liturgies. The law of life precedes the law of prayer, just as the law of prayer precedes the law of belief; just as the law of belief precedes the law of observance. Life comes first: the life of a people, inhabited by the Spirit of life. Life requires concrete and finite forms. But life, though it requires forms, is prior to forms, and outlasts them. Life grows into, alters, cracks, and discards its concrete forms as butterflies discard cocoons.

The Church as institution is secondary to all the Catholic people. The Church as institution is a means, an historical, limited series of concrete forms. The choice before the Catholic people today is what new means they wish to create, to put in the place of the outmoded, encrusted, cracking institution they inherited. The present institutional structure might be destroyed and still the people, as a people, could endure. People first; Church second.

5

Distinctive Traits

UNDOUBTEDLY, there is a tension between "being a member of a people" and "being a member of an institution (Church)." The problem is to state the tension correctly.

The usual apologetical move is to distinguish the "invisible" from the "visible" Church. But that move fails.

First, it does not do justice to a Catholic's responsibilities in the present. The real tension is not "visible-invisible" but "enduring people-changing institutions." Institutional forms are created by those people, for various purposes, in various contexts. No doubt, institutional forms are always inadequate, imperfect, etc. To admit to such a timeless, metaphysical inadequacy is to grasp a truism, but to shed no light on the future.

The responsible questions are: "What are the concrete inadequacies of our institutions now?" "What new tasks should we assign them?" The concrete political problem the Catholic people face in every generation is how to reform (or how to revolutionize) the concrete institutional forms they themselves, by their wit and their inertia, have invented. The enduring people invent institutions as they need them.

Secondly, "visible-invisible" is not sufficiently sensitive to history. For what counts is not the visibility but the historicity of institutions: the precise form taken under given pressures, in specific contexts, for defined purposes. The key questions are: "For what purposes did our people invent the institutions we

now labor under?" And: "What does the present historical moment demand of our powers of invention?"

Thirdly, "visible-invisible" is empirically misleading. For *both*
the people and the institutions are visible, now as in the past. It
is a truism that the inmost heart of men is invisible except to
God. The instructive point is that many who intend to belong to
the concrete, *visible* Catholic people of history are, quite *visibly,*
at odds with the *visible* institutional structure of the Church in
their time. It is the people, in such a case, who hold priority.

A people, of course, is constituted by shared acts of consciousness, by a community of meanings. The Catholic people have
developed in history a dynamic constellation of attitudes, orientations, expectations, and sensibilities, which are in some large way
distinctive among the world's historical peoples. It is this community of shared meanings that is prior to all ecclesiastical politics.

If the Catholic people cease to have confidence in popes, cardinals, and bishops, and find their theological nourishment elsewhere (as millions do today), then the political power of popes,
cardinals, and bishops dwindles into a mere façade. A change in
consciousness forbodes a change in polity. (Politics begins in acts
of meaning. A strong waft of meaninglessness renders impotent
even the most powerful political forms.)

Still, there are many who, in the crisis of meaningless structures today, intend to remain faithful to the Catholic people.
Their problem is one both of destruction and of invention. It
must be admitted—although many have not faced the fact—that,
in some large and significant degree, the structures of the present
Church must be destroyed.

However, it is far more important to announce that the structures of the future Church demand of us fresh powers of invention. Invention is both more necessary and more difficult than
destruction. Invention belongs to creativity and to love and to

being, whereas destruction can be carried by resentment, pettiness, hatred, stupidity, and senselessness.

Still, Charles Davis and others are correct. We must not hide from ourselves the fact that those who wish to invent new concrete structures are implicitly dedicated to the destruction of the structures of the old era.

What criteria shall we use for deciding what structures to put in their place? Are there criteria for distinguishing what is genuinely Catholic from what is not?

It is quite understandable that those in charge of the present structures, because of their own biases and interests, should insist upon their own importance, necessity, and exclusive right to decide what is Catholic and what is not. They have assumed institutional power. No one should suppose that they will relinquish it freely.

To be quite blunt, the Vatican curia is the last of the ancient monarchies. Its power derives from acts of consciousness, not from armies. There is no Bastille to storm. The only plausible way to overturn this inadequate monarchy is to withdraw from it one's freely given credence; to ignore it; to begin building up alternatives. There are many who work upon the great act of altering the institution from within. And the biases and prejudices of those who run the institution have discredited it so severely in the last four years that they have become the principal agents in its dissolution.

Think for a moment of the average Catholic's relationship to his bishop. When was the last time you yourself received a religious insight from, or shared a Christian experience with, your bishop? Is it not true that your bishop has taught you absolutely *nothing* that is now significant in your daily life as a human being and a Catholic? Bishops simply are not leaders of the spirit.

When is the last time you heard your bishop on the radio, saw him on television, read a letter from him, spoke to him? And did you come away with new mind, new heart—or with sadness, disgust, anger?

The institution has lost credibility. As the actual, empirical agent of the spirit of the Catholic people it barely exists. It is a dysfunctional residue of our past. Still, we do not expect our bishops to be the first to announce their own mummification. They must be very lonely men, with a massive sense of helplessness. (Compassion, the Beatles advise, for Father McKenzies.)

Those whose loyalty is to the Catholic people recognize, in the daily contacts of everyday life, that to be a Catholic is different from being a Jew, or a Presbyterian, or a Lutheran, or an atheist. Their memories, sensibilities and expectations have a different shape, a different ring. They find in themselves resources of life that others do not share. They find in others, to be sure, resources that their own traditions lack. They learn from others. But they also learn quite profoundly (though often inarticulately) that they have a distinctive horizon of their own. They sound chords in the universal concert that, apart from them, no one else will sound.

For two reasons I do not think it is profitable at this historical moment to try to state exactly what the criteria are for being a Catholic. In the first place, we have barely explored the character of our own horizon. We have just begun to experience a worldwide sort of pluralism, such that many of us have a prolonged opportunity to live among men of other horizons than our own. By learning to enter their horizons, we for the first time are getting to sense the distinctive contours of our own. We have barely begun to become aware of all the precise differentials in experience, sensibility, and imagination that go into "being a Catholic," as distinct from being anything else. The simple descriptive, phenomenological task has hardly been begun. The subsequent task of precise understanding would, therefore, be premature.

Secondly, the horizons of "being a Catholic" are, accordingly, undergoing change. For a people advances in history. If it is creative, it does not stand still. It changes and grows. It encounters new experiences; invents new images; gains new understandings; makes new, fuller, and more accurate judgments; takes new decisions. We are able today to let into our original, limited horizons vast ranges of material from other world religions, from new technological possibilities, from new intercultural penetration. We ought to expect the Catholic horizon we have inherited to expand, to assimilate, and to undergo transformation. "Growing up into the stature of Christ" is, after all, to grow up into a universal horizon commensurate with that *Logos* "in whom, by whom, and with whom" were made all cultures and all historical possibilities.

At the present historical moment, the establishment of criteria for "being Catholic" is premature; our intentions can be more modest. It will already be a great advance forward if we can obtain a firmer grasp upon our own distinctive horizon; if we can move from simply experiencing it to articulating it. It would be still more impressive if we could plunge more deeply into our own distinctiveness so as to come to the living sources that, far below the surface, were the energy by which it was propelled into the concrete, historical shapes it has assumed.

For there seems to be a paradox in the acquisition of a universal horizon. One does not attain such a horizon in one fell swoop, abstractly, through some universalist common denominator. (There appears to be among world cultures no such universal "Reason" as *les philosophes* and the Stoics imagined.) It seems, rather, that the way toward union with men in other cultures lies through the deepest possible penetration into one's own culture.

One goes to others not by way of a premature universality but by way of a committed particularity. It is as though the world's cultures are one (if at all) in the deepest, most intimate levels, not in the uppermost, most general, most common levels. At the heart of every culture lies an experience of darkness, the experience of nothingness, and therein the discovery of humility and brotherliness: that "humble charity" of which Zossima spoke, like the Buddha, in *The Brothers Karamazov*.

What, then, are some of the distinctive particularities of the Catholic people? It is crucial, at the moment, to identify distinctive traits (if any) on the level of the sensibility, the imagination, impulses, instinct, expectations. For the existential form of "being a Catholic" has not, in fact, been thematized. Formerly, our preoccupation was with abstract formulations, with *theoria,* which we intended to be understood within the context of our own historical experience and imaginative forms. Thus, we defined "Catholic" in terms of cognitive beliefs in doctrines symbolized by Latin abstractions: trinity, incarnation, transubstantiation, infallibility, assumption. But it is the liability of abstractions that, separated from their experiential and imaginative context, their point cannot—simply cannot—be accurately grasped.

And thus we are discovering today that what makes the Catholic people distinctive cannot be intelligibly stated if stated abstractly; one must call to mind those orientations, attitudes, expectations, experiences that shape and fire the imagination in which understanding occurs. The present most pressing specialization in theological inquiry lies on the level of experience, not on the level of understanding. (The liturgy no longer provides the required experiential context, because it does not truly spring from our experience but is the inherited, now abstractive form of the experience of former generations.)

The question must then be phrased differently. *Not:* "What are the criteria (cognitive) for separating what is truly Catholic from what is not?" *Rather:* "What has been the historical constellation of imaginative forms that have shaped Catholic expectations, orientations, experiences? What are the contours of the Catholic imagination?"

I believe that at least the following motifs need to be described experientially in their peculiarly Catholic forms: (1) a social sense; (2) the expectation of evil and pettiness in men; (3) a sense of the absurdity and darkness of life; (4) a zestful acceptance of power and its ambiguities; (5) joy in partial goodness, honesty, freedom, love; (6) delight in the pleasures of the flesh and the palate (wounded where Jansenism lives); (7) stubborn attachment to *theoria* intellectually, but to the modesty of *prudentia* in politics; (8) in married love and daily life a sense of hard-headedness, limits, and tolerance for failure; (9) hope, even zest, under the most severe crises (*la provvidenza*); (10) an exuberance for and generosity toward the arts, sacred and profane; (11) a sense that politics is the penultimate realm (not truth but *maya,* illusion) such that the ultimate test of the politician is his willingness, not to succeed, but to bear witness (the "ultra-resistance"; More; Becket); (12) anti-utopianism; (13) suspicion regarding enthusiasm; (14) a taste for solitude, silence, and contemplative prayer; (15) a respect for the lifegiving power of forms, formalities, routines, and repetitions; (16) a respect for play, festivity, orgy, and fantasy; and several others.

The only way to treat experiential matters is by indirection, by metaphor, by the music and feeling that words invoke but do not state. The following chapters attempt this lengthy task.

6

Searching Time and Memory

THE years that pass since the end of Vatican II are easy for me to remember: our first child was born one day after the Council's end. The Council's first fruit, we laughed at the time, our minds on other things but the poor ending in Rome.

The years since then have been full of turmoil: Charles Davis left the Church, Jacques Maritain denounced the progressives, Gregory Baum moved from a narrow biblical-liturgical orientation to the discovery of secular sociology and psychology. Many conservatives became in churchy matters far more free—William F. Buckley, Jr., and Garry Wills, for example. Many progressives became so involved in the problems of "the church and the modern world," and particularly in politics, that secular problems and political passions became their chief nourishment. Race and war seemed more worthy objects of human struggle. Interest in incessant cases of suppression, violations of free speech, and coldly conscientious exercises of episcopal authority began to wane: the pattern was all too familiar, as enduring as the thick walls of ancient Rome.

Each of us has had to thread our way through this time as best we might. Gregory Baum and Charles Davis have helped us. No doubt each of us can recall a tangled autobiography since that fated December 8, 1965.

"It is my thesis," Gregory Baum wrote in *The Credibility of the Church Today, A Reply to Charles Davis,*[1] "that what

[1] New York, 1968.

Charles Davis describes as the ills of the institutional Church is an outline of the social pathology that threatens the Church and every institution in the world." Again: "The crucial difference between Davis and myself lies in the evaluation of Vatican II." Baum interpreted Vatican II as such an extraordinary thunderbolt that "the entire teaching of the Church" must now be seen in a new focus. Whatever Catholicism *was,* now everything must be seen in a new light.

It was open for Davis to argue that Baum's interpretation, however common among liberal Catholics, does not represent the mainstream of Catholic life and theory; that Baum writes as if the Catholic should leap from St. John the Evangelist to Maurice Blondel while hardly pondering the embarrassments in between; that the "Oath Against Modernism" is a better guide to official teaching than Baum's imaginings; that the "Syllabus of Errors" and all those papal encyclicals down to the present moment, not excluding the textbooks duly established in seminaries during the last five generations, represent a world-view astonishingly different from that proffered by Baum; that, in fine, Baum's view is attractive but unofficial, highly selective, and manifestly in conflict even with many texts from Vatican II.

The two interpretations, of course, require one another. And it is curious to see to what an extent the differences in interpretation are due to temperament, bent of mind, and standpoint. Davis was strong on "consistency" and "logic," and he was after his conversion what he was before: a good articulator of the logic *within* a certain viewpoint. At the time of writing *A Question of Conscience*[2] he was not as good at seeing things from several different viewpoints, or at comparing viewpoints. Baum, by contrast, likes to talk about life rather than about theory, about

[2] New York, 1967.

dynamism rather than about static categories, about mystery rather than about logic, about living rather than about language. In a certain sense, Baum does not take written dogmas or received institutions with the finality that Davis does. When dogmas or institutions are out of line with the Christian Gospel, Davis seems shocked and Baum seems secretly pleased: both find their instinctive theories thereby confirmed.

Baum makes two chief contributions to our discourse about the meaning of the Church. First, he distinguishes seven senses of the word "church" as employed in major documents of Vatican II; the seventh meaning he unseals is that "church" comes into being whenever men are reconciled and human community is furthered. Secondly, Baum notes that we must be careful concerning which sociological model we choose for "church," and he points out the serious deficiencies in using "city" or "state" as a model. His own proposal, that the most useful model is that of a voluntary association, "a movement," stimulates the imagination even though it is not quite convincing. A movement is characterized by a more or less tightly organized and professional center, plus a wide range of ways of belonging to it and assisting its purposes. But "a movement" does not quite suggest the solidity and age-old endurance we associate with "church." The word "people" might be a better model, with the endurance of the Jewish people even to the present day serving as a type. To be a Catholic, then, is not to belong to an organization; it is more like standing among an historical people. To be sure, the Church is by intention and gradual development expected to become co-terminous with the good of the entire human community; that is to say, the Church is intended to be expansible, to change often, to outgrow its earlier and more limited stages in order to be more worthy of man, who is made in the image of God.

70

Baum is also good in pointing out that the development of the Church and its doctrine is not accurately thought of as organic and homogeneous; rather, it is marked by discontinuities and "quantum leaps." Happenings emerge which were not fully contained in their predecessors. Growth is not logical nor consistent, but surprising, sudden, and unsymmetrical.

The question which one continually encounters today, however, is whether the Church has not outgrown itself; whether, in fact, the Church as we have known it—local community of worship and larger organization—has not become dysfunctional precisely because it has been successful. It sometimes seems that all those values and ways of living and modes of responsiveness that Christian teachers constantly instruct us in, verbally and otherwise, appear to be so deeply rooted now in parts of our culture that they are accessible outside the churches, with less artificiality and less semantical and historical ambiguity. A passion for justice, a realism regarding power and achievement, honesty, brotherliness, gentleness, meditative prayer, joy, a sense of God's healing presence and other similar values are as open to non-Christians as to Christians. One does not have to go to church to learn them, to reinforce them, or to celebrate them. One might possibly—even probably—learn them more sharply, more concretely, and more limpidly outside the churches than within.

What shall we say, then, of the argument between Baum and Davis? One's response must inevitably reveal one's own identity; there is here no "objective" point of view, even in pretense. To my mind, Baum's judgment is a little too romantic, too steeped in biblical and liturgical images, too nourishing of a piety and an attitude and a way of life that seem to be less and less valid. When all is said and done, the most important tasks which Baum sets for the Church are now thought of as secular tasks: the building of community, reconciliation, brotherhood. The religious language that Baum employs is now too frequently used as a language of domination and oppression: Christians who talk about "the servant Church" seem to be used as a cover by a church which does relatively little to serve men, or even to accept the language of service. (Not to mention that paternalism is possibly implied in the language of service, anyway.)

On the other hand, the kind of orthodoxy argued for by Charles Davis and the "consistency" he loves so much have been hateful to me for many years. I seem to have had to fight my way out of those issues at so young an age, without help, that I can hardly bring myself to go over them once again. Once one has become convinced that the vast majority of the leaders of the Catholic Church, despite good will, have acquiesced in the mutilating of Christianity, one no longer takes them seriously. My faith as a Catholic does not depend on what the "social structure" of the Roman Church does or does not do. One's task is to assist, at least by a little, in changing that structure.

For to be a Catholic is to stand among an historical people. The task is to open up as many avenues toward an enlarged human sense as possible, to get outside the walls of parochialism and narrowness, to live out in one's own experiences new ways of being a Catholic, to appropriate as many new and diverse experiences as possible in one's own name and thus in the name of one's people. The task is to expand Catholicism to the dimensions of a new humanity, a humanity suggested in Jesus Christ and revealed also (though ambiguously) in every event in history. One can safely forget ecclesiastical language and concentrate upon the rich humanism of the American tradition. Yet even in this concentration, the community established by one's historical people comes as a blessed aid; for not everything American is holy, nor everything modern sane.

Davis says he is "outside" the Church, but remains a "disaffiliated Christian." Baum thinks of himself as a professional, Catholic theologian, in a "movement" rather than an organization, attempting to give all the doctrines, attitudes and ways of life of Catholics a new focus in a new age. I ply my trade as a sometime philosopher, sometime theologian, deriving nourishment wherever I find it, having precious little to do with the organized Church, feeling somehow both blessed and cursed in finding myself a Catholic, both blessed and cursed in finding myself an American. My main focus is not the Church, but what it is to be alive in our time. Still, the Catholic people are the ever-present background of what I do. I cannot think without roots.

Thus I find myself driven back more and more into the origins of my views about man. This search "in time and memory," as John Dunne calls it, is not merely an exercise in nostalgia. ("NOSTALGIA ISN'T WHAT IT USED TO BE!"—a graffito on 72nd St.) At a certain point, one discovers that certain values dominate, not exactly one's thinking, but one's sensibility. It becomes necessary to search out how one came to be that way.

*   *   *

It was, I think, during my freshman year in college that I decided to read every word that Jacques Maritain had written. I was in a Roman Catholic seminary, then, on the campus of a small liberal arts college. My imagination and mind were supercharged in those days: I can remember walking through the fields on the way to class in love, under the screaming blue sky, with God and his world. My heart sang in the way Maritain's prose sang. The earth—and the October red maple tree alone in the meadow, where someone had affixed a crucifix—pointed to God; the earth was alive with analogies. What Gerard Manley

Hopkins wrote was true: a plough makes even earth shine: cleaving exposes beauty. It was easy, then, to say, as Ivan Karamazov could not, "Yes" both to God and to creation.

Maritain blew my mind. I had been brought up in a conventional Catholic household, not Irish, however, but Slovak. There was in our home an affective warmth, a non-defensiveness about the faith, that I was later to miss in Irish parochial schools and parishes and seminary. (On St. Patrick's day, in order to take the special celebrations in good grace, I became "O'Novak"; in the sixth grade I learned to dance the Irish jig for Father Brady's anniversary skit. I remember winning the hundred yard dash on "Irish day" at Kennywood Park in Pittsburgh, my pockets full of free tickets for the amusement rides provided by Father Hannon. Entering the "House of Horrors" I put my arm around blond Elizabeth Flynn, wondering what Father Hannon would think; someone saw me, so later I found out.) On the other hand, the reading matter that came into our house was awful: *Our Sunday Visitor* full of articles about making converts and the horrors of Communism; the *Register,* with its cartoons of dragons labeled "secularism" and its aversion to whatever Eleanor Roosevelt stood for.

Somehow, nonetheless, I had always had the conviction that Catholicism was radically at one with the true and the good. A great deal was wrong with contemporary Catholicism; I knew that from the way my mother and father talked (my mother went to high school, my father to the sixth grade; he got his high school diploma through home courses ten years ago). When I left for the seminary my father said: "Don't let them put you on a pedestal. Always remember you're still a man. Watch out for what they'll try to do to you." He also told me I'd never hear a lecture on the priest as servant to his people; he was right.

I entered the seminary, at the age of fourteen, with more than a touch of skepticism. I found many good things, and good people. I learned to pray, and learned a great deal, as well, about my own conceits and flights from truthfulness. But I also found a kind of death in the Church, a malaise, even a betrayal—now habitual rather than conscious—of basic Christian values. I made a distinction between true, real, lived Catholicism and typical Catholicism; people like Dorothy Day and Baroness von Hueck, whom I made a point of visiting when driving through New York on my way to college, represented the former and the vast majority the latter. I judged "the professionals," clergy and religious, on an especially taxing scale.

Maritain broke in upon my world just when I required a theory of the fundamental obligation of Catholicism to a more general truth and beauty and goodness, needed a lever against falsity and distortion and mediocrity. Moreover, although I was prepared to hate scholasticism and its empty rigors, I had the good fortune right from the beginning of having a teacher (Father Richard H. Sullivan, C.S.C., one of my "real" Christians) who took me, not to textbooks, but to primary sources. I discovered a way of reading Aquinas which armed me against much that passed for scholasticism, "Thomism," or even Catholicism in our intellectual universe. Maritain gave me a way of relating my discoveries in the medieval world to the contemporary world: a theory of art, of politics, of social reform. "It is vain," he wrote, "to assert the dignity and vocation of human personality if we do not strive to transform the conditions that oppress him." Moreover, Maritain sang the praises of the human body (I remember reading, concomitantly, a book called *My Friends, the Senses*). He was, long before the hippies, a devotee of contemplation. "Before being exploited by our industry to our use," Maritain had written in *True Humanism* (1936), the earth "demands . . . to be familiarized by our love." Earth, cornstalks dying under a silver moon, the caw of the crow, sweat, and human seed: God speaks in everything.

Because of my promises of celibacy, I could not at that time seek the human love I very much desired for sharing these discoveries. My joy, however, was not diminished; it was heightened by the sense of doing what I wished to do, and at some cost, and by having to find other ways to express the affectivity I felt. Here, too, Maritain was of assistance. His poetic sensitivity, his own creative drive, but above all his renowned gentleness and openness to people served as a model at which, however remotely, one might aim. The experience of reading, at nineteen, *Creative Intuition in Art and Poetry* is one of the most intense and beautiful that I recall, even though now on perusing the book I am, disappointingly, unable to recapture the fervor of those days. Once and for all that book freed me from the tyranny of words; I recognized that there are many operations of intelligence besides those which are verbal, or as I was taught at Harvard, "cognitive." And I learned to search in writers for precisely those apperceptions which cannot be said and (as Wittgenstein later put it for me) must be shown.

Maritain also provided for me an intellectual path for moving from the political conservatism of my home town to liberalism—not, to be sure, the usual American liberalism of, say, Stevenson. The tradition Maritain articulated made the liberalism of John F. Kennedy resonate for me as it could not, quite, for the editors of *The New Republic:* a liberalism not of the Enlightenment but of more tortured ages, tutored by a sense of evil, absurdity, and tragedy, and unafraid of the compromises and complexities of power.

In today's terms, Maritain was more "New Left" than "liberal"; questions of value were prior, in his mind, to questions of function. "Justice," he wrote in *The Range of Reason* (1952), "is not simply a table of technical adjustment and material improvement. It requires an idea of the dignity of the human person, and of the spiritual value of justice, freedom, and neighborly love." Moreover, Maritain had an attractive ability to assimilate: "I am glad to be Voltaire's debtor in the matter of civil tolerance, or Luther's in that of non-conformism, and for these things I honor them; they belong to my cultural universe."

I learned soon enough that secular intellectuals did not find in Maritain the liberation that I did; on the contrary, he was for many proof of the irremediable medievalism of Catholicism. (One remembers Morton V. White's typically condescending and ill-tempered review of Maritain's *Moral Philosophy*.) Even, it turned out, Catholic intellectuals in Europe disdained Maritain and his neo-Thomism; lionized in America, he was considered second-rate in France. The new directions were biblical studies, phenomenology, anything but scholasticism. Still, Maritain was for me, as I believe he must have been for very many others, the means of liberation, the poet and philosopher who taught us that "the seven centuries of laziness" must be ended and fresh intellectual strides taken. The Church is not what it is today, it is what it must be tomorrow: our loyalty is to the Church reformed. And, on the other hand, we cannot pretend to belong to a different Church than the Church of today: God speaks in this very moment, in the gnarled hands of the peasant saying his beads, despised by liberals, in front of tiers of flaming candles.

Consequently, I am obliged to wrestle hard with Maritain's reaction to Vatican II Catholicism. I read *The Peasant of the Garonne*[3] with nostalgia, with affection, and with gratitude. In it I see the route that I have traveled and I see that Maritain, who

[3] New York, 1967.

77

pointed, has not himself traversed the whole way. The book, even in the controversy it has stirred, is a testament to the immense progress made by Catholics in these last ten years. Maritain, who was once a leader, has fallen back. He shows us with long-suppressed bluntness (the bluntness of his early books on Bergson and *Three Reformers,* softened in middle age, has returned) what he cannot understand. And what good are giants if we do not mount their shoulders and see what they did not?

Maritain calls this his last book and asks frequent pardon for his advanced age, for the pose of the blunt peasant, and for a magisterial and at times insufferably pretentious tone. Reading this book is like returning to one's father's house to find him less than himself. Too frequently, Maritain quotes from previous works, for as much as a page at a time. The last sections of the book are woven around long passages quoted from books, manuscripts, and letters of his departed wife. One feels immeasurable sadness in seeing a man betray, in the end, the vision and the vigor that had characterized his life.

For it is not that the task Maritain has undertaken is unimportant. Possibly, those who are not Christian, nor even believers in God, are in a position to see that task more clearly. (Atheists are today the guardians of Christian orthodoxy.) How many have not wondered whether modern Christians, in their enthusiasm for "relevance," are not simply evacuating traditional Christian themes of all significance? How many have not smelled the fishiness of many efforts to make Christianity conform to the standards, tastes, and needs of various influential sub-groups of the modern period, especially the intellectuals and the myth-makers? How many believe that behind the front of "reform and renewal" is hidden a profound loss of life, the advance of an unadmitted atheism, the larvae of *mauvaise-foi?*

Maritain is offended by the "Christian tomfoolery" of the present day. He does not take back his past contribution to the effort at a genuine *aggiornamento;* again and again he notes the immensity of the task and the scarcity of laborers. Moreover, he gives brief, sharp analyses of what was ailing Roman Catholicism in the nineteenth and earlier twentieth centuries: he still understands the laziness, the complacency, the hatred of the body, the error that this world is to be despised, the unsavory alliance of theological and socio-political conservatism, the immobility of imagination and conception, and, above all, the craving for security. His pages on integralism, on the failures of Thomism, on Jansenism, are as devastating as any he has ever written. He says plainly that his is still a heart which, by temperament, "is of the left," and that in the social and political bearing of the Church he is much more often with the left than with the right. He dates (and applauds) the sundering of the confusion between the interests of religion and those of a certain privileged social class, in which there thrived despite its religiosity a "comfortable practical atheism," with the founding of the review *Esprit* in Paris, in 1932, and of Dorothy Day's *Catholic Worker* in New York at nearly the same time.

After his dissection of integralism, Maritain sees that, "With a crash, the pendulum is swinging to the opposite extreme." Having suffered himself the integralist "methods, accusations, and denunciations," he hopes not to lose his head over the change, and not to yield "to the delicious and so 'consoling' pendulum movement which is sweeping along so many of my dear contemporaries."

Maritain has a passion for Truth (duly capitalized). In philosophy and in theology, he serves no other master. Moreover, he sees this truth through a tradition of discourse that he discovered in Aquinas, not as though Aquinas had invented it alone, but as though it were a "living organism built up by the labors during three thousand years of thousands of thinkers, known and unknown," which Aquinas "brought to a unity." Aquinas, Maritain thinks, established the model for any future intellectual *aggiornamento;* he established, as his medieval biographer puts it, "a new method, new reasons, new points of doctrine, a new order of questions." He saved the truths of the past; he entered into and wrested from controversy and confusion new truths from his erupting, creative environment.

Thomism is, in Maritain's view:

an intelligible organism meant to keep on growing always, and to extend across the centuries its insatiable thirst for new prey. It is a doctrine *open* and without frontiers; open to every reality wherever it is and every truth from wherever it comes . . .

Maritain can imagine Thomism seeking out other matrixes of inquiry "in other universes of thought formed under other heavens."

I like to imagine all that could be brought to us by a Hindu who had become a Christian and a disciple of St. Thomas, and who would thoroughly know, with a kind of piety and filial connaturality, the Vedantic schools of thought and their particular ways of intellectual approach.

He imagines Thomism free of St. Thomas, too, "as he was in himself, and ready, like him, for the changes and remodelings required by a better view of things, and for the enlargings and deepenings demanded by an inquiry that is always going forward."

Maritain makes it abundantly plain that there are two unshakable experiences at the center of his moral life. One is his act of faith in the Church; the other is the ineffable experience, penetrating ever more deeply into his consciousness, and finally conceptualized as "the intuition of being." Concerning the Church,

Maritain has a simple, humble, obedient faith of which, among younger philosophers and theologians, I do not know the equal. With greater equanimity than they, Maritain seems able to note and to digest institutional sins and inadequacies, and to discern even in untoward and evil deeds some working of the Holy Spirit. When he says "Church," he says something at once mystical and realistic. He pays the verbal formulae of the Church a great seriousness. Younger theologians, less certain of how precisely to discern the Spirit in the interplay of historical and institutional argument, approach more cautiously the language and symbols used by the Church during its various epochs. They do not have—they are certain it is not right to have—Maritain's literal certainty.

Concerning the intuition of being, Maritain tries once again to evoke for his readers what cannot be said. Twice (pp. 132–135 and 137–139) he tries to clarify what he means and to block misunderstandings. Contemporary Anglo-American philosophers are not sympathetic to appeals to personal experience, even if Maritain is calling attention to *their* personal experience. Moreover, Maritain's basic metaphor for this intuition, "seeing," and even the word "intuition," are both misleading. His second treatment makes that plain. There he appeals also to "listening," to "allowing to emerge," and to many other metaphors. The fact is that there is nothing to "see" or even to "hear"; being is not an object which suddenly appears upon some screen of consciousness.

What is intended by the phrase "intuition of being" is a decision (which, for various reasons, feels right to us) to accept as valid the fact that when we claim to know p, at least two conditions must be met: (a) we are in a position to know p, and (b) we can supply evidence supporting our claim to know p. When these conditions are met, the knowing subject is claiming a relation to the evidence; self and evidence (in most cases and to

81

some extent independent of the self and not manipulatable) are united in one act of consciousness. To become aware that to say "is true" or "is the case" is to claim some unity between consciousness and evidence, is to have taken the chief step toward Maritain's version of "realism." The intuition of being is not, properly, an intuition but a reflection upon our activities when we claim to know, and what such activities imply regarding the relation we assume toward the world. For Maritain, it is cause for surprise, wonder, and marvel that knowing occurs; that subject and evidence meet, mutually constituting the act of knowing.

Maritain then takes a further step, in asserting (from our daily, ordinary practice) an isomorphism between human consciousness and the world. It is true that we do act *as if* inquiry led us to a more accurate knowledge of our world, *as if* our constructions progressively revealed to us "the world as it is." But—once one leaves behind the common-sense world—one cannot help wondering whether such constructions, even the most scientific, are mere tales told by idiots, signifying nothing. One lacks the certitude that Maritain feels in his "intuition," the at-home-ness, the sense of fraternity or family feeling he has for the universe. One feels the world may be more chaotic, mad, and at loose ends than his serenity allows. The Lord, after all, may be Lord not of the ordered Hebrew-Greek-Christian cosmos, but, as in Raymond Nogar's title, *The Lord of the Absurd*.[4]

It is, in another sense, Maritain's sudden lack of serenity that is most disturbing. To be sure, Maritain is concerned lest other Christians, especially professors, kneel so devoutly before the spirit of the present age that they "leave three things behind": the other world, the cross, and sanctity. I wish he were living now

[4] New York, 1967.

in America, and could feel the passionate quest of young people for holiness: reverence for themselves and others, joy, freedom, and a moral integrity strong enough to resist immense social pressures, middle-class conditioning, and prison itself. I wish he could taste the evil young people have encountered in our society, and share in their experience of redemptive suffering. I wish he could fast with them, wear sandals with them, embrace the poverty of resistance with them. I wish he could rejoice in their discovery of contemplation. I wish he could hear their biting rejection of "the spirit of the age." I do not think our secular society yields to a Christian society in its sanctity. The young may not appeal to the symbol of the cross (in fact, many of them who are not Christians do), but many understand its meaning.

It is true that in attention to the "other world" the Christians of this age are deficient. But no one can do everything; Christians in every age have been deficient. Medieval Christians could do little to change the conditions of life in this world; their imaginations were excited by the next. Our task is different. We would consider ourselves deficient were we to do, in our situation, as little as medieval men did (Aquinas included) to alter life on earth. The favorite text of many of us has become: "Eye has not seen, nor ear heard, nor has it entered into the mind of man to conceive" what eternal life might be. We take the hint and leave that issue to God, and meanwhile concentrate upon those secular actions with which "eternal life" is consistently linked: feeding the hungry, clothing the naked, comforting the sorrowing, teaching the ignorant. This is, we believe, to seize the point.

Belief in an afterlife *is* waning; little emotional or imaginative emphasis supports it. Yet it still seems to many good to live as Jesus lived. If it turns out that death is not, as it appears to be, annihilation, that will be God's surprise; meanwhile it seems good to labor to diminish, as Camus said, "at least by a little the number of those who suffer."

In his earlier days, Maritain would not have done quite so much preaching about the immense task of "discernment and integration" that needs to be done, nor quite so much carping at his fellow laborers, of whom there are so few. And he would not have rested so comfortably upon positions he had achieved two or three decades earlier. Many of us have had his warnings fixed in mind. Many do not like Teilhardianism any more than he does. But, then, an old peasant has a right to speak his mind, and it becomes the young to offer him an ear; mocking him occasionally as he mocks them.

The errors of the recent past, Maritain writes, are no excuse in the present for fatuity, mental weakness, or mental cowardice. ". . . the amount of foolishness and intolerance in human history remains relatively constant, merely passing from one camp to the other, changing styles, and having significance in terms of opposite algebraic signs."

But the problem with which Gregory Baum, Charles Davis, and all of us labor is to "redeem the time"—*this* time, not some other one, and to read the changing signs correctly.

7

Voice: The Unspeakable

MANY of my friends, as Maritain urges, are in fact beginning slowly to return to wisdom learned from "the three m's": monasticism, mysticism, and the middle ages. When astrology comes back, can mystery be far behind? The limits of verbal, conceptual, analytic speech have been explored and penetrated. Most of the matters that concern our identity cannot be said in words.

At Notre Dame, Frank O'Malley for many years taught a course on "Modern Catholic Literature." The influence of that course has spread all around the country. Two of O'Malley's students, Fathers O'Donnell and Keena, introduced me to writers I had hardly known existed. One of the characteristic concerns of such writers was their argument against a thin modern rationalism, against objectivity, against what came to be called "the Houston style": the secular, pragmatic, profane urban man. Often these writers were romantic. Sometimes they were reactionary. Always their criticism was radical.[1] They taught me unforgettably, especially the novelists among them, the power of what cannot be said.

There is something mysterious about fiction that cannot be spoken of in the categories of ordinary psychological analysis, perhaps cannot be spoken of at all. I find I can perceive it—I listen for it, I can hear it come on strong, falter, fail—but I am

[1] See Richard Griffiths, *The Reactionary Revolution,* New York, 1965.

85

uncertain how to name it or how, even, to tame it, to make it lie flat and be examined. The quality I am thinking of has long been, for example, Graham Greene's strong point (as it is of all memorable, re-readable writers). At present, I call it "voice." It is a little like music, but it is more than rhythm, melody, tone.

Voice, perhaps, is in advanced societies part of our forgotten language. Commonly, we find ourselves trained to disregard it. On listening to a lecturer, we feel constrained to evaluate his performance—no, his words—coolly and objectively. Dispassionately we point out his mistakes of fact, lapses in logic, and analytically we distinguish his presuppositions, adducing reasons why he should have included others or erred in the ones he assumed. We repress the way we reacted to the grinding of his voice, his egotism, the stiffness of his gestures, his sweating face, the corners and angles of his metaphors, emotions, aggressions, his gentle humanity. We discount his subjective qualities and our subjective reactions. We swiftly pass over the antagonism (or sweetness) that arose in our stomach. We step outside whatever spell he cast. We proceed with impersonal rigor.

All these reactions, I have come to think, fall far short of those to be expected from a fully developed human personality; all are signs of underdevelopment. It is not true that having set aside the "mythical" responses and the "metaphysical" responses of the human organism, and entrusting ourselves to the "objective" or "positive" responses, as Comte simply and others with more nuances have urged us to do, we enter into a higher stage of human development. We impoverish ourselves. People in other, more "backward" cultures, and the poor and the white lower-middle classes in our own country (those toward whom we educated ones nourish such missionary feelings), are not infrequently more "advanced" in the perception of voice than those in whom it has been, by a distorted scientific training,

86

rigorously inhibited. What potty training does for later sex life, disciplined objectivity does for perception of voice.

Voice is that quality in speech or in writing which takes up lodging within us, as a participation in our "stomachs" (the Karamazov seat of intellection) by the "stomach" of another. I do not say that voice "conveys" another's distinctive horizon (sensibility, imagination, understanding, judging) to us. That way of speaking implicitly suggests that others are separated from us by some gulf across whose silence and emptiness messages must be conveyed. Such an image of the situation might be called the individualistic bias. A more accurate image of the relationship between human beings is that we already live in one another, already participate in one another, inhabit together a common cultural matrix; we are far more communal than we are individual, far more part of one another than distinguishable from one another. You are already I, I am already you, before even a word is spoken, a written word read.

Voice, then, is the quality by which we recognize the other already in ourselves. It is the capacity of the spoken or written word to make our own interiority light up with the joy of perceiving what, in any case, was already true: that others do inhabit us, we are far more united than our ingrained prejudices (in an Anglo-Saxon, Protestant, Enlightened world) allow us to be always conscious of. We fancy ourselves atomic individuals, separate and alienated ("othered"), when the truth is astonishingly far from that. Voice is the lighting up in us of distinctive, individual, unmistakably unique accents which we already know without knowing, participate in dimly but not consciously. For the paradox of tradition and the individual talent (T. S. Eliot) is that a distinctive unique artistic voice is (in that precise measure) wholly communal. Our community is rich; virtually infinite our species. All of it lives primordially in us. The artist awakens that voice of his in us which we already have long, though dimly, heard.

Thus artistic merit always comes by way of surprise and recognition. Surprise, because the usual clichés of our awareness separate us from large numbers of the human race, find us living on too few cylinders of our true identity. Recognition because the race is, after all, one and mysteries of our natural participation in one another remain to be plumbed. Moreover, artistic merit is distinguishable from pretended art (from trash, from "popular novels") inasmuch as its works bear re-reading. They do not merely distract; they awaken, restore, reveal to us ourselves, touch nerves distractions overlay, or daily grind has dulled.

The writer who, surprisingly, taught me about voice was Graham Greene. Among writers of fast-paced stories, Greene could easily have become a mere distractor. His facility at the hard, shocking, but finally dulling perceptions—the clang of rain on a metal roof in the tropics, the crack of pistols, sad romantic sunsets—could have won him a large popular audience, not quite a class of re-readers. But Greene early caught the Victorian bug of the great English novelists. He awakens in us echoes, dreams, sadnesses, beginnings. Through a whole series of books he has found a haunting vein in our—forgive the metaphor—cultural soul. Childhood and dream; loss of a mother and recognition; pity for the innocent, uncared-for, white dressed girl in her teens; the long sadness of middle age (hardboiled, secure, vulnerable, near tears). And yet, even my putting these floating images in words falsifies them, for it is not merely by the construction of visual images, not by sounds or metaphors or scenes of emotion that Greene moves us.

His secret is the rhythm of his sentences, some incantatory magic in which connotations, accents, alliteration go straight to our stomach. I pick up *Travels With My Aunt*[2] to give an hour to it. I can't put it down. It is one a.m., two a.m., finally three and I am finished. It was not the suspense, not the "action," not the inherently interesting characters, not the amusing and incredible vignettes (O'Toole counting how many seconds a day he spends pissing, totalling the amount in one year; old, sick Uncle Jo on the upstairs floor, pulling his grating suitcase behind him with his cane, dying with triumph). I asked myself again and again, what is pulling me on?

Greene at his best (confident, easy, unafraid to reveal himself) constructs a dance of metaphors—scene, characters, incident, plot—to distract the conscious mind. It is a little like all those exercises of meditation and contemplation I practiced for so many years: composition of place, re-play of a dramatic action, bait to keep the imagination busy. The real prayer was going on much more deeply in the psyche. It was a quiet stream, wordless, a fundamental attitude, a willingness, a listening. Those are the depths whence voice arises. (A six-month tour through *The Ascent of Mount Carmel* would distinguish, in medieval language, the levels of the soul.)

The drama inherent in the story is a powerful metaphor for what is going on in the lower depths; but it remains that, somewhat separate, a bait, an excuse. The dream has its own slipstream, the story provides tasks for the language to perform while a dream is woven.

Sometimes, the voice lapses. The first scene with the young girl Tooley—eyes too heavily made up, bright-eyed, tender, troubled—falters. There was an old dream here; an old trick that no longer carries the voice. With the old woman, Aunt Augusta, the writing is different. Every sentence registers inward.

[2] New York, 1969.

What does it mean? What is the message? In a sense, such questions overlook the forgotten language. They linger in the bright, clear light under the lamppost where we have been taught to play. The "message" of the book—convention requires one, Greene supplies—is that a staid, dead banker finds new life in sin, illegality, danger of death, and Paraguay. England as bourgeois death; Africa, Latin America, Asia as dangerous life: an old Greene message, at the structural root of his work. But such "messages" are trivial. (Even in Norman Mailer, they are trivial; it is not "the white negro," vitality arrested from conformity, that is of interest, but Mailer's tormented, indecisive voice.)

Voice is not meant to be stated. It is what is not stated. In a sense, it is not even (hateful word) "communicated." It is participated in, mutually lived, the least sentimental love, the one non-saccharine community. "Do I hear you saying . . . ?" people (grotesquely) say, when they do not in fact participate in the voice.

A most unsatisfactory way to criticize fiction, is it not? But C. S. Lewis was probably right when in *An Experiment in Criticism*[3] he said that the present fashion in criticism—analysis in order to conclude: "This is bad because . . ." —is both un-literary and destructive. The test of good reading is whether people who love to read in fact re-read it. And they will do that, I argue, if the voice rendered in it is a voice they cannot bear living without, a voice they want to return to, because it awakens streams in them they want to keep running clean and strong. Those who are ready hear; those who are not, do not.

The narrator of *Travels With My Aunt* says of himself that he has lived too deeply in the Victorian world, the age of the

[3] Cambridge, England, 1969.

great English novelists, to be suited to the modern world. He estimates that his sensibility would probably be ranked, were he a writer, not with the giants (Dickens, Austen) but with the minor writers (Stevenson, Defoe) of the period. That is another winning feature in the voice we learn to hear; it stirs in us emotions we know to be truthful, in tune with who and what we are, like lost echoes of a childhood, lost unities, lost peace.

Voice, I say, cannot be stated. It is revealed through style—a word that like so many others today needs to be redeemed. "Style" has become a vehicle for sentimentality ("new life styles," "the Kennedy style"), a substitute for thinking. Still, Kennedy *was* a Catholic, and his emergence (coupled with the rise of Jewish writers) made such differences as those between a Catholic and a WASP tangible. The emergence of the word was inevitable.

8

Style

STYLE is to role as existence to essence. What is the role of the Christian in the modern world? The question supposes that there are abstract norms, abstract laws, accessible to the Christian (or applicable to him) and perhaps to no one else. What is a Christian style? The question asks about the concrete bearing of this man engaged in this action in this situation. The question asks whether this man is *graced*: is there a gracefulness to the way he performs, a beauty, an unstudied but discernible *éclat*? "Grace," Bernanos warns us in the last line of *The Diary of a Country Priest*, "is everywhere."[1] Grace is not confined to Christians. It is the shining forth of beauty in action. Peguy had caught it in one of countless historical moments, in one of its familiar and perhaps too churchly forms:

> [God speaks:]
> When once you have known what it is to be loved freely, submission
>   no longer has any taste.
> All the prostrations in the world
> Are not worth the beautiful upright attitude of a free man as he
>   kneels. All the submission, all the dejection in the world
> Are not equal in value to the soaring up point,
> The beautiful straight soaring up of one single invocation
> From a love that is free.[2]

But grace also has secular forms. Rieux, the secular saint, swims

---

1 New York, 1956, p. 253.
2 "Freedom," *Basic Verities,* Chicago, 1965, p. 135.

in the shining sea off Oran and tastes the joy of living; then in the fetid plague-ridden streets of the city he acts with dignity and compassion, in communion with all men who suffer.[3]

Christians have not adequately reflected on the meaning of the opening lines of St. John's Gospel: "In the beginning was the Word . . . and in Him were made all the things that were made." Jesus is the Logos, the symbol, the model, the concrete style, in which this creation—out of all possible styles—was created. There are, then, two different ways to learn about Jesus: through the man born in Bethlehem and dead on Golgotha and risen at Easter; and through the things made in his image: all cultures, all places, all times, all persons, all things. We do not, until the end of history, know all that is to be known about the Word. For not until history is complete will the concrete style of its unfolding be complete: will the full Word be spoken, and all things have yielded up the image in which they were made.

Hindus, Mohammedans, Buddhists, and atheists, in discovering that honesty, compassion, and vision are key human values (the "golden rule," Erik Erikson[4] tells us, is universal) do not name Jesus. But they do name effectively the empirical correlatives[5] to which Christians point when they say Jesus. Jesus is way, truth, life, love; he is understanding and loving. Atheists understand and love. How can any man avoid the concrete style imparted to the real world of history? One does not have to be a Christian to be realistic. There is only one world, equally accessible to all men. If Christians are correct, that world is made in the image of Jesus. Even if Christians are *not* correct, that world is very *like* the image of Jesus: Any man who commits himself to understanding and loving lives realistically, and any

[3] Albert Camus, *The Plague,* New York, 1948.
[4] *Insight and Responsibility,* New York, 1964, pp. 217–243.
[5] See Anthony Levi, *Religion in Practice,* New York, 1966.

man who closes himself to understanding or loving stunts his own development and rends the tissue of other human lives. There is no escape. For atheist, Hindu, Buddhist, Mohammedan, Jew, and Christian, understanding and loving are basic. The style of this particular creation demands them, and suffers when they are absent.

First corollary: Christian knowledge of the Word is stunted because Christians have so far confined their thinking (out of arrogance) to the thought forms of Western Europe. They have scarcely begun to listen to the Word revealed in Eastern or African cultures. As missionaries, they have gone not to learn but to teach. Yet the Word is revealed in all cultures. One preaches the gospels by recognizing what is already revealed in the Samaritan, the Centurion, and every person one chances upon. Before speaking, one listens. All the more is this true today when, as information, the "good news" has already gotten around. By now, everyone knows that there are Christians (white men who build empires and think that God became man, died, and rose again). The trouble is, the medium is the message. Empires tell of Christendom, not Christianity, and myths of racial superiority distort the listening and the dialogue. Wisdom should speak to wisdom, abyss crying out to abyss, mountain to mountain; instead, the white man preaches and has no ears. The Word goes unheard. The missionary enterprise has been misconceived.

Second corollary: Christianity introduces into history not so much new facts, as a more precise interpretation of history. There are four fundamental human operations which constitute an individual's "horizon," the range of all a subject can perceive or do.[6] These operations are: (1) experiencing; (2) understanding;

[6] See Bernard Lonergan, "Metaphysics as Horizon" in *Collection,* New York, 1967.

(3) verifying; (4) deciding. These four operations are dynamically related: (1) experience raises questions for (2) understanding, which provides hypotheses that need to be (3) verified; and verified judgments raise questions about what the subject is (4) going to decide to do about his knowledge. A horizon is less than fully realized until the cycle is complete: a man is subject to criticism for deficiencies in any of these four operations. In terms of these operations, Christianity presents itself as a light for (2) understanding and a strengthening of (4) the willingness to act. Occasionally, Christianity may introduce men to (1) new experiences, but by and large any given human experience—of conversion, of community, of penitence, etc.—occurs among other men too. Experiences vary from temperament to temperament, culture to culture; I doubt that there is any specifically Christian experience.

But the *interpretation* given to basic human experiences may be Christian. Christians are inclined to *understand* their experiences in the light of the classic form of the life of the historical Jesus: losing life and gaining it, exodus and promise, death and redemption. But it would be a mistake to think that other men are blind to occurrences of redemptive suffering, or to the yielding of autumn and winter to the spring, or to the transmittal of life from aging parents to youthful children. The style of creation is Christic, whether Jesus is known and named or no. The style of the historical Jesus is crisp and clear, and it reveals the nature of God and the destiny of man in a lightsome way—and one remains a Christian if and only if that light seems brighter than any other. Yet this light is not an exclusive, rather an inclusive, light. Other cultures may know more about the Word in whose image all things are made than Christians confined to Western ways of understanding Jesus. Jesus—the historical Jesus—will not be completely known until all nations have absorbed his witness and discovered riches which only they are sufficiently endowed to detect. When the Word is completely known, only then will the historical Jesus be completely known. Western Christians have a very narrow purchase on the revelation of the Word. Hence their present embarrassment and the glaring nakedness of their arrogance.

Third corollary: it is illegitimate to speak of others as "anonymous Christians." Rather, all men are equally searchers for the full revelation of the Word. Scientists trace his tracks.[7] Those who build cities pursue the possibilities enfolded in our fecund and developing universe. The dualism between secular and Christian is untenable, for all things reflect the Word, all are holy, and holy not in some "added" way but simply in being themselves. We are all "anonymous humans" until we each speak the word groping for articulation through our destiny, until all our words in concert form the text of the Word in history: the story complete. We are members of each other as words of a sentence. The "mystical body" of Jesus is the total story of human history. It is brotherhood in a plot intricate, bloody, tragic. It is by no means a pretty morality play. It is realism with a vengeance, real life in its complexity, a world in which children die screaming in the night.

Fourth corollary: the question is put wrongly if one asks, "What, then, is the advantage of being a Christian?" Christianity is not the opiate of the proletariat nor the LSD of the suburban, white middle classes. Christianity does not function to fill human needs, as if the lack of Christianity makes a man less than human. Christianity offers light on the real lot of men: good things must die in order to live; men learn only by paying the

[7] No one has seen this point better than Teilhard de Chardin, especially in *The Divine Milieu*, New York, 1962. It is easy optimism I object to in some Teilhardians.

price of blood; life is cruel and unfair—and yet fecund, creative, onrushing, leaping from scheme of probabilities to scheme of probabilities in contingent, open-ended, developing fashion. Men must take responsibility for life. Christianity offers no escape from history. It insists that men must accept responsibility, enter the darkness, take the risks, die, and perhaps never, themselves, see the fruits of their labors. Its criterion of success is not utopia but integrity in action. We are called, not to succeed, but to labor. It happens, as a matter of fact (it is the style of the real world), that creativity springs from such sources; seeds fall into the ground and die.

Fifth corollary: Bonhoeffer erred in turning in a Barthian direction.[8] This means that he put too much trust in the historical Jesus, and not enough in the Word revealed in all places in history. Bonhoeffer was correct in discerning a "religionless Christianity" but wrong in pressing all history into the mold and pattern of Jesus. Rather, he should have turned to the variety of this world to discern the Word, and thence come to an ever more profound penetration of the yet unknown Jesus. It is not as if Christians already *know;* it is, on the contrary, that the glass through which they look is still too culturally narrow, small, and one-sided. But even when the glasses of all cultures are assembled, they are still dark. Hence, the atheist faithful to the darkness—to Camus' "polar night"[9]—also tells the truth about the Word: it shines in a darkness not to be dissipated. Perhaps for this reason Bonhoeffer[10] could speak more honestly of God to atheists: God is spoken of truthfully only in darkness,

[8] "The world's coming of age is then no longer an occasion for polemics and apologetics, but it is really better understood than it understands itself, namely on the basis of the Gospel, and in the light of Christ" (*Letters and Papers From Prison,* New York, 1962, p. 200).

[9] *The Myth of Sisyphus,* New York, 1960, p. 48.

[10] *Op. cit.,* p. 165.

and those with pretensions of *knowing* (what Kierkegaard[11] called pagan "recognition") not only do not know but cannot receive the light. Those who "receive the light" are those who, unable to know if they love God whom they do not see, love their neighbors whom they do see. Atheists do this. Which does not make them "anonymous Christians" but changes them from "anonymous" to "authentic" human beings—a transformation at which even a Christian might say: "For me the beginning of life."

It is weak usage, then, to speak of "a Christian style" or even of "Christian styles." Style is personal and concrete, not general and abstract. The style is the man. Those who imitate the style of John F. Kennedy, or James Bond, or Humphrey Bogart, or Marlon Brando, do not have style; they are playing a role. Too many Christians play at being Jesus, and that is why there is so much falseness in Christian life. To imitate Jesus *with style* is to be faithful to oneself as Jesus was faithful to himself; it is not to copy him; it is to be different from him. Before playing at being "a man for others" one must be sure to be oneself. A man alienated from himself cannot be present to others, nor can he act with style, nor can he be in his context what Jesus was in his.

Not a great many persons have style, because too many persons play at various roles and never fashion their own genuine identity: allowing it to express itself from within, in spontaneous response to others. People play too many games with one another. Original sin is the mythical description of the fact that people are born, as Eric Berne[12] says, trapped in games of their parents' contrivance. A game-free life (another name for grace) is rare;

[11] See the appendix on "Childish Christianity" in *Concluding Unscientific Postscript*, Princeton, 1964, p. 531.

[12] *Games People Play*, New York, 1964. See the beginning of the last section, pp. 171–184.

even the best of human beings are only relatively free. Style arises from the struggle of each person against himself, the struggle for liberation.

Such a struggle is not, be it noted, narcissistic; it is communal. In this sense, style is a gift we give to one another. For only those who have been loved—who have received what Erik Erikson[13] calls "basic trust"—are capable of loving others. Only those who can love others can free themselves from themselves. Only those who can thus be aware, free, and other-centered can achieve a style. Others are confined to playing roles—playing professor, student, preacher, professional Christian, village atheist, angry young man, defender of the American way of life, and the rest. "How to become free?"—The same question as: "How to develop a style of my own?" (The answer is not: Rebel. Neither is it: Conform. The answer is a secret which one must in part discover and in part invent for oneself.)

Style is to role as existence to essence. Writers on ethics find it easier to talk about roles—which may be described and sometimes are normative. But the real trick to ethical living (as Aristotle[14] saw) is not to cover all the ground with general laws, but to touch the ground. Every ethical agent is unique; every situation is unique. An action is not moral insofar as it is the instantiation of a general law; morality does not arise from generality (Karl Rahner[15]). Morality arises from "hitting the mark"[16] in the concrete—from doing the right thing at the right

[13] *Op. cit.,* pp. 69, 79, 179–80, etc.
[14] *The Nichomachean Ethics,* Rackham translation, Loeb Classical Library, Cambridge, Mass., 1962, p. 75 (Bk. II, c. 2); see also p. 87 (c. 4, 5–6).
[15] Karl Rahner, "On the Question of a Formal Existential Ethics," *Theological Investigations,* Vol. II, Baltimore, 1963, pp. 217–234.
[16] See *The Nichomachean Ethics,* p. 93 (Bk. II, c. 6, 9–15; VI, c. 9, 6; etc.) My interpretation of these passages is in *The Experience of Nothingness,* ch. 3.

right time, in the right way, with the right motive, in a right reading of the needs of others, etc. And for this there are no general laws but only that kind of ethical insight which is able to "hit the mark" exactly, missing none of the demands of the concrete. Yet such insight is not acquired hit-and-miss; a lifetime of liberation[17] from one's own pet games is required before one can see situations as they are, rather than as one would wish them to be.

Hence, past experience and patiently acquired general laws and rules-of-thumb[18] are normally required if snap judgments are to "hit the mark" with higher frequency than they miss. A man familiar with the situation at hand is more apt to "hit" than the new arrival. But all this is by way of probabilities: in dealing with the concrete, not certainty nor necessity but statistical probability is the maximal expectation. General laws are illuminating and may frame the background or the context of most ethical decisions; but at the point of contact with reality an ethical decision is unique and falls under no general law at all.

Others conform to laws—usually by rebelling against laws; the good man extends the realm of sensitivity and goodness beyond the law. The pseudo-good obey the law. The restless, the rebellious, and evil man (the immoralist) spurn the law and in its place supply a game of their own. The pseudo-good have security; the restless, the rebellious, and the immoralist seek fun; the truly good have style. (Sometimes the immoralist, in shocking the pseudo-good appears to be doing evil when he in

[17] See Bernard Lonergan, "Ethics as Liberation," *Insight: The Study of Human Understanding,* New York, 1957, pp. 619–626.

[18] See the extraordinary essay by James M. Gustafson, "Context Versus Principles: A Misplaced Debate in Christian Ethics," *New Theology, No. 3,* New York, 1966, pp. 69–102.

fact is doing good—which is why the immoralist, much more often than the pseudo-good, has style. He, at least, is at moments faithful to himself.) In our day, there are so many pseudo-good that the immoralist performs a necessary ethical function; he clears the air and inspires the drive for fidelity to oneself and others which leads to genuine morality.

Style, then, is the grace which comes from freedom—the freedom to accept oneself as one is, and others as they are; the freedom to cease pretending; the freedom to meet the real world as one wishes, when one wishes; the freedom to enjoy the challenges, the roadblocks, the ironies, the tragedies, of the real world as it is. From such freedom flashes a beauty, a peace, a power that add gracefulness to good performance. Some who have had style in our day are Albert Camus, John F. Kennedy, Pope John XXIII, Paul Tillich, and (in his own stiff, German way) Dietrich Bonhoeffer. In the wake of persons of style come imitators, playing the latest role. Thus every new style is experienced as a liberation, only to end as imitation: existence is reduced to general laws, described, made normative.

"Be yourself" is not only a Christian imperative. It belongs to all men. That is why grace is everywhere. What Christianity adds is the following illumination: When you are most at one with yourself, you will find that the revelation of the Word makes more sense as an interpretation of your life than you perhaps had thought. There are many ways by which to come to the revelation of the Word, however. Some who go by way of reflection upon the things that are made travel farther than those who go by way of the historical Jesus. That is why all men need one another, and why Christians today feel so close to atheists: They have stopped their incessant preaching and begun to listen. The same Word speaks in all places, in man's strength and in his weaknesses, in wordlessness and in words.

Protest is not a necessary factor in the achievement of style, except insofar as the preachers of essence wax stifling and oppressive. Again, it is possible to protest too much, a common fault among those who, even while reacting against it, more than half believe what the preachers of essence say. Such preachers are clearly wrong. No need, then, to protest too much. Only to go about the business of being free, the business of fashioning a style, the business of becoming a man. It is difficult to fight one's way out of playing a role, even the role of being a Christian. Those who try this path soon learn humility, for the risks are many, the self-deceptions frequent, and the way dark. But at least they will later say: "I lived my own life." Who does that has style.

And also?—is dwelt in by God. Perhaps. God is not an alien, but closer to us than we are to ourselves. To speak at last in our own true voice, to have achieved a style of our own, is to manifest to others that presence of God unique to us. Even to pray is, in fact, to seek one's own genuine style;—and to seek that style is, possibly, to pray.

9

Prayer

EVER since the death of God, prayer has come to seem useless·
Or perhaps it is the other way around. How, in any case, ought
a mature man to pray? Now that men do not "need" God, and
God is quite clearly no *deus ex machina,* how can men pray?
In his last hours of life Dietrich Bonhoeffer was seen kneeling
silently in prayer. What, then, is the role of prayer in a "world
come of age"?

It is astonishing to discover, in frank ecumenical discussions,
how many Christians no longer pray—I mean silently, by themselves, with regularity, for a protracted length of time. It is, by
contrast, sobering to find that a lecture to a secular audience on
prayer, particularly on mystical prayer, brings students to the edge
of their seats—they have never heard anyone speak of the kinds
and types of prayer, and of the practical difficulties and obstacles;
their own contemplative instincts are stirred. One discovers soon
that atheists and agnostics among the young have devised their
own ways of satisfying these instincts. They seek solitude and
quiet frequently. At other times they prefer to meditate on profound themes with others, to the accompaniment of quiet instruments or the reading of poetry. They already have experienced
the fruits of contemplation; they are surprised to find a Christian
tradition articulates some of their own experiences. Ordinarily,
for nourishment they have turned away from activist Christians
to the contemplative East.

Many otherwise sophisticated Christians, it seems, are extraordinarily naïve in their understanding of prayer. They have scarcely progressed from the habits of childhood. When they become adults, they put away the things of childhood, including prayer.

To be sure, the prayer of children can be genuine prayer. Prayer is for men of all ages, and so there is a childish form of prayer suitable for children. Children treat God as they treat their fathers and mothers. The mode, quite simple, is "Gimme," and it is only with some effort that children can be made to remember "please." The tragedy is that many Christians retain this attitude all their lives. For many centuries Christianity has been paternalistic in mode and the Christian people have been allowed, and sometimes even encouraged, to remain childish. Kierkegaard describes the result in a devastating analysis called "Childish Christianity" in his *Concluding Unscientific Postscript*.

We should not be surprised to learn, then, that many Christians today think that prayer means asking for things; for good weather for a ball game, to find lost objects, to help our elected officials, to pass an exam, to find a parking place, to obtain peace of mind, to make an important sale. The mode is "Gimme." The implicit world view is magical: as if one who prays were at the center of the universe, as if the function of God were to hurry about tending to needs which human beings are powerless to satisfy for themselves. God becomes, like a father, a Great Need-Filler. He does what we cannot do for ourselves. When we cannot explain things, we supply "Providence" as an explanation. God becomes, in the slightly more offensive phrase, Big Daddy.

But if petition, petulance, and the need for functionaries characterize the life of childhood, what characterizes the life of adults is reconciliation with the real. The real is not the *status quo.* The real world is a dynamic, open-ended scheme of events in which the future emerges from the present according to the interacting series of probabilities affected by the past and the present. To be reconciled with the real is to be willing to change often; it is to be pointed toward the future, struggling to realize those probable series of events which commend themselves to a good conscience, and to oppose those which do not. It is to be sensitive, alert, aware of alternatives, and willing to take responsibility for one's decisions. To be reconciled to the real is to *enjoy* the risks, decisions, and responsibilities of creating tomorrow by one's actions today.

The form of prayer suitable for adults, therefore, is a form of prayer that is open to the future, that brings the one who prays under criticism, and that prepares him to act even when he does not yet know the complete outcome of his actions. This form of prayer was simply expressed by Mary at the Annunciation, and by Jesus both in the Lord's prayer and in the garden of Gethsemane: "Thy will be done." Ivan Karamazov said that he could not say Yes both to creation and to God at the same time. Essentially, the heart of genuine adult prayer is to say that Yes. The essence of prayer is a Yes: to God and to the real world as it is.

Prayer, then, is fundamentally an orientation of the will. It cannot be primarily a product of intelligence, for the intelligence is not master of the future, or even of the present or the past. Just as the scientist hopes to find an answer before he finds it, so a believer in God prays even though he does not see God. There are many things in life one does not understand. Events are often cruel; good things perish easily, and evils multiply swiftly. Many things in the world do not seem as if they are godly, let alone redeemed. In prayer, one does not pretend to understand. A man at prayer merely asserts that he is open; he is ready for more; he is still *disponible;* he will assume responsibility for doing what he can to realize the possibilities, however limited, which still lie open to him. Even in a concentration camp, a man can pray; prayer is the last activity to go; it is the innermost citadel.

In this sense, the basic form of prayer is, "Let it be done to me according to Thy will." The "it" is an unknown; it is an *X*. What the future holds, or what will be the actual results of one's present decisions, it is impossible to predict with certainty. Human understanding is never adequate to the complexities of contingent, concrete living; we understand thoroughly neither our own motives, nor the fullness of the present situation, nor the reverberations of our actions in the texture of future events. Nevertheless, we must act. In adult prayer, we are not shifting our responsibility onto God; we become conscious of our limitations and learn the joy of risk and choice—the joy, in the face of uncertainty and ambiguity, of creating. In adult prayer, we accept the burden of creating the unfinished world in a darkness in which we cannot see fully what we are doing.

Consequently, the fundamental act of prayer may be virtually wordless. Prayer is an attitude of radical openness. Since the *X* for which one prays is unknown, one does not have to formulate strategy, tactics, or objectives (though these have their place). One has merely to achieve a basic willingness; one opens oneself, affirmatively, creatively, toward the unknown—toward whatever God might ask.

God, of course, does not speak to us through a little voice in our heart; people who hear voices are not, generally, to be trusted. It was the solid teaching of St. John of the Cross that one should always presume that voices, signs, visions, feelings, or the like, have natural causes. God ordinarily works in ordinary ways; we must not expect magical interventions. God speaks to us through the persons, places, situations, and events which form

106

the concrete texture of our lives. We should not listen for the voice of God over and above the sounds of the real world. God (if there is a God) speaks with the voice of real events; God speaks in a wholly secular way. Whatever happens, that is God's will. We know what God wills to happen only *ex post facto.* To speak of God at all is to interpret what happens as if it were known and desired by one who calls us his friends and even his sons; but one must believe this interpretation in the face of everything that happens, however evil, neutral, or "secular" it appears. In any case, the Christian adult's energy is wasted if he looks for God; ordinarily God makes his will known only in real events, and one might as well, therefore, concentrate on discerning what actually is happening in oneself and in the world.

Moreover, even when we pray for things that we desire, we should recognize that our desires are known to God before we articulate them in prayer. To desire is already to pray; even to breathe is to pray, for to breathe is to accept the future and to step forward. Besides, as Gabriel Marcel remarks in his chapter on prayer in *The Mystery of Being,* a man does not live as an "I" but as a "we." In prayer, all those others who make up the texture of one's intersubjective life are also present. All those whose lives affect ours—all who speak our own language and transmit the wisdom and limitations of our culture, and all those whose opposition challenge us—are present with us. Thus the image of other persons can never be a "distraction" at prayer; they are part of our prayer. To pray is to become aware that one is not at the center of the universe, but that the universe has many millions of conscious centers of aspiration and action. To pray is to heighten one's sense of reality; above all the reality of other persons.

Finally, the effect of prayer is not that it binds God to something. God is not our servant-boy, to be summoned and given orders. The effect of prayer is to change ourselves. It is to make us more alert to the subtle nuances of human relationships, to the actual course of daily events around us, to possibilities for creativity and brotherhood to which we have been blind. The function of prayer is to free us from institutional prejudices and inherited routines, to help us to become spontaneous and—in Eric Berne's phrase—"game free." The reason for praying is to become more realistic, more open, more discerning. It is not even necessary to employ the word "God," and it is certainly not necessary to imagine someone out there (or deep inside) listening to us. It is only necessary to say yes to reality, and to go back into the complexities of history with a renewed sense of compassion, honesty, self-criticism, and openness. Reality makes many demands upon us; the purpose of prayer is to open our eyes and ears to the fullness of the real world in which we live. This is why even atheists pray frequently, without ever thinking of "God."

As for believers, they do not see the God to whom they pray. When they are trying to be faithful to the demands of reality, it is God who is the "light" within them—the very force of honesty and courage in their hearts. To give rein to honesty and courage, through a free act, for the sake of brotherliness, is to live in God and God in self. Such life *is* God's life, no other.

10

A Fresh Conception of Theology

THE fact that it is difficult, even embarrassing, to speak of God in many modern contexts is not, then, a criterion for the elimination of all speech about God. Relative to certain standpoints, it may be unintelligible, inadequate, false, or even morally blameful to speak of God; from the standpoint of scientific method, for example, or from the standpoint of magic and superstition, or from the standpoint of one who has no experience of or insight into any referent for that word, or from the standpoint of those who have heard that word used as a cover for injustice, dishonesty, obscurantism, and moral complacency.[1] Nevertheless,

[1] Thomas J. J. Altizer has written: "Our task is to strive to discover a language which cannot be spoken by the forces of domination. Here, an easy pragmatic test might be: a theological word or phrase is illegitimate if it can successfully be employed in a political speech, an advertisement, a television serial, or in any institutional statement whatsoever. If only on the basis of this test, many of us have decided that 'God' must be dead, or our faith is in vain. . . . To speak the name of God or the promise of God or hope in God at a time when God at best can be known and envisioned as the totally Other, or most easily and immediately as an alien and oppressive Other, is to sanction the alien otherness of our time and our world with the sacrality of the divine name. . . ." See "Commentary on Michael Novak's Essay," *The Religious Situation* Boston, 1968.

The hope for such a test seems to me too frail, since no human words are safe from misuse; *corruptio optimi pessima*—but no way has ever been discovered to prevent the corruption of the things most dear to us. The announcement of the Death of God has also been made into a slogan. Consequently, I imagine that the theologian, like the poet, is constantly *purifying* words, *recovering* lost meanings, *breaking through* to new

it may be true that there are standpoints from which the employment of the word "God" is both intelligible and justifiable. Moreover, it may be true that among such standpoints are standpoints it would be wise or commendable for at least some human beings to take in addition to or in preference over other standpoints.

Our discussion of prayer leads us to a new conception of theology and suggests that the present distinction between philosophy and theology is obsolete and inadequate. It may help now to summarize rapidly the lessons which the radical theology of Thomas J. J. Altizer and William Hamilton has taught us; to draw from them, however, a somewhat different moral than those two authors have themselves drawn;[2] and to move then to the larger context of the contemporary university. For the problem of theological method is a problem faced by the humanities and the social sciences generally. It must be solved on a level of generality and more fundamental analysis than that of theology alone. In particular, I want to propose the notion of *a theology of the open standpoint*.

I.

The proposal of radical theology is bold: Christians should attempt to work out a Christian theology without reference to God. Just forty years ago, English philosophers were making a proposal about philosophy that was almost as bold: philosophers

---

usages, *redeeming* abused language, *inventing* fresh combinations. The word "God" seems to be hopelessly lost today—to make it *mean* again can probably best be done by silence and indirection, and also by returning, like the poet, to the living founts of personal and communal experiences.

[2] *Radical Theology and the Death of God,* New York, 1966; Thomas J. J. Altizer, *The Gospel of Christian Atheism,* Philadelphia, 1966.

should attempt to work out a philosophy without reference to any subject matter; philosophers should concentrate upon the analysis of language and the elimination of verbal puzzles. In both cases the proposal was disturbing, paradoxical, and revolutionary; one would not at first believe that it could be carried out. In the case of philosophy, the revolution in question quite clearly has borne valuable fruit.

Radical theology goes to the heart of the matter. It forces theologians to search for an adequate methodology. Moreover, by its concentration upon the central concept "God," it insists that this search not be superficial or peripheral. Radical theology has called the emperor naked; it has confessed that even the inner consciousness of theologians is secular. It is no longer possible to imagine that faith lives in one hermetically sealed container, as if Christians well knew what they believed and their only problem were how to communicate this belief to others. The problem is that Christians themselves do not know exactly what they believe, or why. The problem is radical. The fruitfulness of radical theology lies in its rejection of the three theological programs which preceded it.

(1) The first program was that of theological liberalism. Liberalism embraced secular methods of historical and literary inquiry; envisaged Christianity as the cutting edge in the general secular progress of the time; tried to interpret theological statements as statements about human drives, needs, experiences.

(2) The second program was that of neo-orthodoxy.[3] Neo-orthodoxy made revelation its basic category; turned in disillusionment from the liberal myth of progress and saw Christianity as a judgment upon and a scandal to secular society; and tried to interpret theological statements as statements about a non-

[3] See James D. Smart, *The Divided Mind of Modern Theology, Karl Barth and Rudolf Bultmann, 1908–1933*, Philadelphia, 1967.

111

empirical "encounter" either with the "Wholly Other" or, more exactly, with the Christ announced in the bosom of the Christian community.

(3) The third program was that of "depth" theology (Eliade, Buber, Tillich).[4] Depth theology maintained that modern secular methodologies treated man too superficially and, specifically, failed to notice the question of meaningfulness, of mystery, of ultimate concern at the heart of human consciousness; saw in the destructiveness of the twentieth century proof of the inhumanity of the modern secular, technical mode of consciousness; and tried to interpret theological statements as statements answering to the depths of man's needs and aspirations.

Radical theology has rebelled against these three preceding programs in something like a reverse order. Against depth theology, Hamilton and Altizer wish to strike a note, not of anxiety and metaphysical concern, but of exaltation and liberation.[5] They feel the force of at least one form of modern secular consciousness.[6]

[4] Langdon Gilkey, "Social and Intellectual Sources of Contemporary Protestant Theology in America," in *Daedalus* (Winter 1967), pp. 69–98.

[5] See "The New Optimism—From Prufrock to Ringo," *Theology Today* (January 1966), pp. 479–490; reprinted in *Radical Theology and the Death of God*, pp. 157–169. For Bonhoeffer's criticism of Tillich, see *Letters and Papers from Prison*, New York, 1962, pp. 194–198. For Altizer's relation to Tillich, see *The Gospel of Christian Atheism*, p. 10: ". . . it was Tillich who exercised the greatest theological influence upon my work. . . . While I have been forced to resist and oppose Tillich's theological conclusions, I do so with the conviction that they are not yet radical enough, and with the memory of Tillich's words to me that the real Tillich is the radical Tillich. Certainly, Tillich is the modern father of radical theology, and . . . his influence is felt at most of those points where theology is now being carried beyond its traditional limits."

[6] I do not share the view which the radical theologians sometimes seem to share, according to which the criterion for acceptable theological discourse is the standpoint of "modern men." My reasons for rejecting this criterion are two: (1) there are many varieties of "modern men"; (2) ac-

To try to reach the dimension of depth, the experience of encounter, the sense of the sacred, seems to them an artificial, arbitrary exercise.

At the same time, the rebellion of Hamilton and Altizer against neo-orthodoxy is even more marked. The strong sense of a Church community, indispensable for neo-orthodoxy, has been shattered in America; strictly secular questions, outside the context of Christian categories, constantly arise. "Revelation," for example, implies that God reveals himself, and neo-orthodox theologians speak a great deal of "God's actions in history." But suppose one does not experience the "encounter" which alone is said to validate language about God; suppose one tries to stir it up but it simply won't come. The suspicion arises that feelings of

---

cording to a thoroughgoing relativism all standpoints, including the many standpoints participated in by various "modern men," are subject to criticism from other standpoints. It may count against a traditional theological proposition that it is "unintelligible" to "modern men"—it certainly counts against its present usefulness—but it seems wise to assume that men of preceding eras were equally as intelligent and judicious as we. It is only a matter of good historical method, then, to try to recreate the standpoint from which propositions asserted by them made sense to them; one must judge assertions made within one standpoint by the criteria proper to that standpoint. The word "God" has made sense to some people; there are some standpoints in which it has found meaningful employment. The standpoints from which the word is not meaningful are not the only ones, nor are they *ipso facto* superior frameworks.

If, further, one wishes to choose one standpoint over another standpoint, one cannot do so merely by asserting the superiority of one alternative; one must *show* that superiority; for example, by taking account of more data and meeting further questions than can be done from within the other standpoint; or, again, by showing that one can communicate to more people by the employment of one standpoint rather than another; and so forth.

For a similar critique of radical theology, see Peter Berger, "A Sociological View of the Secularization of Theology," *Journal for the Scientific Study of Religion,* Vol. VI, 1 (Spring 1967), pp. 7–8.

encounter may be the product of self-manipulation or ecclesiastical conditioning (the *koinonia*).

On the other hand, the radical theologians do not wish to return to the program of liberalism. To be sure, they, like the liberals, concentrate upon this present world and its sharp taste of reality; the word "transcendent" offended liberal sensitivities and is without meaning to the radicals. But too much has happened in the technology and politics of the twentieth century to allow Hamilton or Altizer to accept the liberal, romantic notion of God as the motor-force of progress and human perfectability.

II.

The problems of theology would be extremely discouraging if the same problems were not facing nearly all the traditional disciplines of the humanities. It must be obvious to nearly everyone connected with the contemporary American university that many among our brightest and most sensitive students no longer share the methodological programs set forth by the generation of professors preceding ours or by ourselves. The humanities seem about to undergo a profound revolution. For the humanities, as we know them, have been largely aristocratic and bourgeois in character. The modes of perception, forms of community, and methods of expression proper to the poor, to "primitives," and to "underdeveloped" peoples are not at present well represented in the study of the humanities. Students who have worked among the poor or in "underdeveloped" nations are not always prepared to admit that the "humanity"—the maturity, intelligence, perception, subtlety—of the people they met there is "less developed" than that of professors in the humanities and sciences.

The wrong conclusion to draw from these developments is that we must simply return to raw experience, or that we should abandon theoretical and technical interests in pursuit of immediacy. The correct conclusion appears to be that the theoretical structure of the humanities and the social sciences (perhaps of the physical sciences as well) needs to be deepened and enriched. A revolution in the intellectual life of a period commonly springs from the introduction into intellectual consciousness of a fresh body of experience. In our case, the fresh experience comes from two quarters: (1) we have for the first time in history begun to achieve international consciousness; (2) we have begun to discover the relativity of our own methods of perception and inquiry and of our own criteria of relevance and evidence. It is probably obvious that these two sources of experience spring chiefly from enormous advances in technology,[7] and that they lead to what Teilhard de Chardin called "the emergence of the noosphere."[8]

A first major result of the new flood of experience has been the re-emergence of theology as a serious discipline on the secular campus, a discipline much sought out by many of the most intelligent and sensitive students. The growing interest in theology seems directly due to the increasingly conscious relativism of our situation; the inadequacy of pragmatism and moderate positivism has become apparent.

If we agree to identify the dominant intellectual spirit at the best American universities during the past generation as a type of pragmatism, characterized by a systematic avoidance of metaphysical questions, a preference for value-free discourse, and a methodology based upon mathematical and empirical procedures, then we might say that many perceptive students, who will go

[7] Herbert W. Richardson, "Five Kinds of Faith," in *Toward an American Theology*, pp. 30–49.

[8] Teilhard de Chardin, *The Phenomenon of Man*, pp. 180–184 and *passim*.

on to become professors, no longer accept this spirit as the regnant spirit of their life. The reasons why they no longer accept this spirit are several: (1) there appears to be no necessary connection between such pragmatism and humanism; and the habit of value-free discourse, in fact, seems to them to dull the perception of values; (2) a refusal to raise ultimate questions makes radical criticism of "the system" unlikely, and the pragmatist seems to be reduced to the role of a technician whose adjustments merely keep the present system running; (3) the symbols, rituals, and spirit of the pragmatic temper do not manifest special cogency in comparison with other possible modes of human life. Many students, in short, are now more interested in choosing a way of life for themselves, rather than merely falling into the pragmatic system and pragmatic style smoothly laid out before them.

To raise the question, "But why be a pragmatist?" is, of course, to raise a question beyond the limits of pragmatism, at least where pragmatism is narrowly construed as a way of life based on the power of prediction and control. To ask the question, "Who am I?" or "What do I wish to become?" may lead to other answers besides the pragmatic answer: "One who gains the power of manipulation over himself, others, and events." The man who thinks of himself as a manipulator even of himself is, in the eyes of many students, alienated from himself in a not especially attractive way. In brief, the model of the cool, detached, hard-nosed, disinterested observer and experimenter— the white-coated expert in his laboratory, or the realistic politician in his office—is losing its hold over the young.

One may deplore this tendency, rejoice in it, or feel ambivalent regarding it. What has been permanently fractured is the pretense of objectivity, inevitability, and prescriptiveness which the scientific-pragmatic temper for so long maintained. A student does not have to take the scientific-pragmatic attitude toward the world. The shaping of his personal identity is a matter of his own choosing. He might, for example, regard the model of the pragmatic man as a suitable model to imitate in *some* situations in human life—where a good tool for instrumental purposes is required—but not as a model for the whole of life.

In any case, a debate is now possible in the minds of the young concerning which models for human life they will choose to emulate. Such a question is a "meta" question. We do not need to call it metaphysics. But it clearly represents a freedom from the model which has weighed too heavily upon our intellectual life for some decades now. The young are capable of detachment from the intellectual standpoint which characterizes most of the professors around them. They are free to choose a "style" of their own.

A *standpoint* is the set of experiences, images, presuppositions, expectations, and operations (of inquiring and deciding) by which men make themselves conscious of their own identity and their relation to their world. It is obvious that a standpoint cannot be exhaustively *stated* in a set of propositions; at best, it can be *shown*. For all language makes sense only from a standpoint; outside that context, its meaning shifts or is lost. Moreover, a standpoint is personal to each man; no two men (for environmental, neurological, and other reasons) have exactly the same standpoint. It is true, of course, that standpoints overlap and that a set of higher standpoints can be participated in by many men, so that a whole cultural period, or national sentiment, or class bias, or intellectual world view,[9] can be characterized as

[9] An extremely clear view of the criteria which govern a very powerful contemporary world view is given by Williard Van Orman Quine: "We can improve our conceptual scheme, our philosophy, bit by bit while continuing to depend on it for support; but we cannot detach ourselves from

representing a standpoint in which many men share. Nevertheless it is also true that each man's standpoint is uniquely his own. When a man *shows* his unique standpoint, furthermore, he manifests *style*. The style is the man. You cannot *state* who you are, what your standpoint is, but by all your words, gestures, intonations, actions, etc., you *show* it. Style (as we have seen) is to role as existence is to essence; it is the showing forth of a standpoint through action.

Given these definitions of standpoint and style, we can construct the beginnings of a method for theology. The first step is to recognize the international scope of contemporary consciousness. Theology can no longer be merely denominational or confessional theology. To be sure, there is still a place for specialists and for those who speak from within one among many theological standpoints. Unavoidably, in fact, each of us does so. Yet an adequate theology today must be able to enter into many historical standpoints, and perhaps to invent other possible standpoints as well. The theologian at his best must operate from a "higher standpoint,"[10] or better, an "open standpoint," free to empathize with, to explore, and to enter into more than one historical standpoint. Otherwise he cannot do justice to the uniqueness and value of each of the historical systems around us.

Here, a *caveat:* It is not necessary for a theologian to pretend

---

it and compare it objectively with an unconceptualized reality. Hence it is meaningless, I suggest, to inquire into the absolute correctness of a conceptual scheme as a mirror of reality. Our standard for appraising basic changes of conceptual scheme must be, not a realistic standard of correspondence to reality, but a pragmatic standard . . . the purpose of concepts and of language is efficacy in communication and in prediction. . . . Elegance, conceptual economy, also enters as an objective." *From a Logical Point of View,* Cambridge, 1953, p. 79.

[10] See Lonergan's "higher viewpoint" in *Insight,* New York, 1957, pp. 13–19, 233–234, 257, 374, 439.

that he has a different history than he does have, or to try to force himself into a style that pretends to be non-historical or supra-historical. To be able to operate from a "higher" or "open" standpoint does not mean to pretend to possess a "superior" or a "detached" standpoint. It means, rather, to be able (within limits) to sympathize with and to understand other standpoints than the one one chooses as one's own abiding style of life. Perhaps we have all met Presbyterians who can articulate a Roman Catholic standpoint better than many Roman Catholics, or Jews who can articulate the standpoint of Buddhism. Standards of sensitivity, fairness, and profundity in such matters are beginning to take shape, although at present it seems difficult to spell them out. There seems to be such an achievement as "hitting off" a standpoint exactly, in tone, manner, feeling, intellectual perception, and theological precision; but it does not yet seem possible to state all the conditions that are met in such an achievement. The best test at present seems to be the approval of those whose standpoint is being expressed by the other.

In brief, to be able to operate from a "higher" or "open" standpoint is a second-level achievement. It is the ability so to be conscious of one's own historical standpoint that one can deal sensitively, fairly, and profoundly with standpoints not one's own. It is a form of historical consciousness, a fruit of the appropriation of one's own relativity.

III.

A theology of the "higher" or "open" standpoint is possible because the root of theology lies in what Lonergan calls man's unrestricted drive to ask questions,[11] in what Tillich calls man's

[11] *Ibid.,* pp. 220–222, 348–350, 380–381, 599–600, 623–624, 636–639, 701–702; see also my *Belief and Unbelief,* pp. 26, 64, 70, 91, 97, 125, 173n.

"ultimate concern,"[12] in what Schleiermacher calls "the sense of absolute dependence,"[13] in what the mystics call "the void."

> On a dark night, Kindled in love with yearnings—
> oh, happy chance!—
> I went forth without being observed, My house being
> now at rest.
> In darkness and secure, By the secret ladder, disguised
> oh, happy chance!—
> In darkness and in concealment, My house being now
> at rest.
> In the happy night, In secret, when none saw me,
> Nor I beheld aught, Without light or guide, save that
> which burned in my heart.
> This light guided me More surely than the light of
> noonday,
> To the place where he (well I knew who!) was awaiting
> me—
> A place where none appeared.[14]

Theology commonly negates every notion, symbol, idea, image, or concept which it employs to express its affirmations. The reason why this is so is that the root of theology does not lie in any one conceptual system, pattern of images, or cultural context. The root of theology lies in a drive in human consciousness to question every fixed or finite symbol. The human spirit appears to be more inexhaustible than any one set of constructs established in history. All historical symbols are relativized in the light of this fundamental drive. On the other hand, some sets of historical symbols may be more adequate than others in allowing this

[12] See D. Mackenzie Brown, *Ultimate Concern: Tillich in Dialogue,* New York, 1965, pp. 7–16.

[13] *The Christian Faith,* New York, 1963, pp. 12 ff., 19 ff., 34, 40, 125, and *passim.*

[14] St. John of the Cross, *Ascent of Mount Carmel,* New York, 1958, p. 12.

fundamental drive free rein. A prophetic religion, for example, seems more likely to change in accord with the demands of changing situations than a religion whose symbols are static. A religion whose symbols are open to other forms of cultural expression seems more faithful to the drive to raise questions than one whose symbols are parochially and irrevocably fixed. Some religious traditions, more than others, may make it easier for their theologians to enter into the open standpoint in trying to learn from other religious traditions.

The drive to raise questions is the principle of ultimacy in religion. Nothing is so sacred that it may not be questioned; not even the concept or name of God is exempted. God in most major traditions, in fact, is the one who cannot be conceived or imagined, the one who is named as opposite to the unlimited drive to ask questions: not to be encompassed by any finite system. From an atheistic point of view, of course, there is no God opposite to our unlimited drive to ask questions; at best, the name "God" merely calls attention to the inexhaustibility of that drive by giving it the sort of shape a name yields. Whether or not the name "God" truly names, whether or not the class is empty, the fact remains that theology springs from the drive in man's passions and intelligence to question the validity of every finite cultural or conceptual system, and to be aware that this drive is inexhaustible. It is quite possible for an atheist to be a theologian.

Yet besides the inexhaustible drive to raise questions, which is the root of all theology capable of an open standpoint, there are also limited, finite religious traditions and sub-traditions: Hinduism, Buddhism, Judaism, Christianity, Islam; and Protestantism, Catholicism, etc. The role of these traditions appears to be that of giving concrete shape and style to the cultural working out of the drive to ask questions. The drive to raise questions is, of itself, unstructured. One cannot raise all questions at once.

121

One cannot grasp the inexhaustible directly. Consequently prophets invent ways of life, disciplines are taught, symbols yield gleams of revelation, cultural events become revelatory signs. One proceeds to the hidden by way of the obvious. Conversely put, one proceeds to the one who *is* by way of the things that are not—to the one whose reality is of a different sort by way of the things we normally call real. Theology is in constant dialogue between concrete immediacy and the ultimate. Its structure is "incarnational" or "epiphanic":[15] ordinary human flesh is the vehicle in which and through which the holy is perceived. But one must be taught how. Theology is an *ascesis,* a learning of the way, the receiving of a gift of light.

Learning theology is, to put it differently, learning how to affirm *and* to deny. For this reason theology is particularly appropriate for coping with historical relativity. The task of learning how to operate from an open standpoint involves learning the relativities of one's own standpoint as well as the relativities of other standpoints. To see fundamental concrete symbols as others see them, and to learn how to discern what is illuminating and what is merely adventitious in such symbols, is a tricky business. Living with relativity requires trickiness.

An example from Christian theology may make my meaning clearer. In the debate between liberal theology, neo-orthodoxy, and depth theology, one of the most hotly contested points concerns how to determine the starting place of theology. Liberal theology wishes to start from human experience, neo-orthodoxy wishes to start from God's inbreaking revelation, depth theology wishes to start from a question in man's experience to which relevation gives an answer. From a higher or open standpoint, each of these approaches is worth trying; each is a response to a

[15] See Ninian Smart, *Reasons and Faiths,* London, 1958, pp. 54–126, 162; see also Ian T. Ramsey, *Religious Language,* New York, 1963, p. 53.

given context; each has advantages over the others; and each has liabilities. More important still, these three standpoints are not the only three human standpoints available. One will also want to listen to the testimony of men who do not accept these standpoints and try to study the symbols and myths they employ. It is not likely that any one Christian standpoint will exhaust all the riches of Christianity, or all the riches of being a man. From the higher or open standpoint, a Christian theology will have increasingly sensitive ecumenical ears'and a more powerful awareness of secular alternatives. It has become impossible to do theology for one's own denomination only, or even for believers only. Increasingly theology is being done with larger and larger segments of the human race involved. In principle, universalist religions like Christianity are open to an ever deepening universal context.

IV.

What, then, is special about Christianity?[16] What about its historical embodiment in the church, limited in time and place? In principle Christianity is intended for all men. It is, to be sure, a religion with a memory, a living tradition, and roots in a concrete historical people. Nevertheless Christianity does not have an essence—an essential core of doctrines, attitudes, or practices,[17] unless in some vague and unsatisfactory sense. Rather, Christianity in history is a series of variations on several themes. There are "family resemblances," as Wittgenstein would put it, between various manifestations of Christianity; there is not one irreducible

[16] See my "Human First, Christian Second," *A Theology for Radical Politics,* New York, 1969.

[17] Benjamin A. Reist, *Toward a Theology of Involvement: The Thought of Ernst Troeltsch,* Philadelphia, 1966, pp. 182–186.

essence everywhere the same. (A sensitive historical sense will show that not even in Roman Catholicism is there such an irreducible essence.) It is entirely conceivable that there could be a Buddhist Christianity,[18] as there is now a Roman Christianity, or an African Christianity as there is now a Nordic Christianity. As we shall see in the next chapter, certain images and symbols may be the constitutive characteristics of Christianity—affecting intelligence by way of the imagination and "ways of perceiving," rather than through concepts or propositions.

On the one hand, Christianity is an historical religion cherishing its relationship to certain concrete places and events. On the other hand, it is an open, outward-oriented religion, capable of adaptation to any historical culture. On the one hand, Christianity has no existence apart from its embodiment in certain concrete cultures and concrete forms of ecclesial life; on the other hand, Christianity is not exhausted by any one concrete culture or any one form of ecclesial life, for it is in principle dynamic and universal, open and susceptible of transformation. The laws of its development and transcultural power have not been worked out.[19]

The Anglo-American philosophical tradition, I would now add, seems to be facing a similar crisis. Anglo-American philosophy is, in fact, one philosophical tradition among many. It sometimes makes claims to a certain universal validity and general superiority. But it has some of the marks of denominational or confessional presuppositions. Its pragmatic bias seems to block dialectical, "subjective" questions about presuppositions. The question "Who am I?" does not play a large role in the tradition.

[18] Dom Aelred Graham, *Zen Catholicism*, New York, 1963.
[19] See, for example, Owen Chadwick, *From Bossuet to Newman: The Idea of Doctrinal Development*, Cambridge, 1957; Reist, *Toward a Theology of Involvement*, p. 37.

The emulation of the physical sciences and mathematics some-times seems to give it the illusory hope of posing as the one true philosophy. The key move commonly made in this tradition is to agree to meet any alternative before the bar of reason, but to define "reason" in its own terms.

Young persons looking on the Anglo-American tradition note, if you will, the pragmatic effect of that tradition in our present society; not a very relevant effect. What philosophers consider important does not always seem important to students. The prag-matic and dispassionate style of analyzing existent language patterns, for example, seems to prevent one from making a radi-cal criticism of presuppositions,[20] on the one hand, and from creating new possibilities, on the other hand. These criticisms may be just or unjust; the point is that Anglo-American philo-sophical standpoints and their corresponding styles are not the only ones presently attracting the young. Relativism afflicts philosophy too.

In the analysis of standpoint and style, moreover, Anglo-Ameri-can philosophy seems peculiarly handicapped. Standpoint and style cannot be exhaustively stated; they can only be shown. It is the manner and bearing of the linguistic analyst, it is his liturgy of language games and moves, it is his symbols of puzzle-ment, clarity, and the untying of verbal knots, that reveal his identity more powerfully than any of the propositions he states. To analyze such matters, disciplines like anthropology and the-ology seem at present better equipped; for they are especially interested in the phenomena of symbol, ritual, liturgy, myth, point of view, and qualities of experience and perception that show a man's standpoint and his style.

A man has only one life to live. He is free, within limits, to

[20] Herbert Marcuse, *One Dimensional Man,* Boston, 1966.

125

choose his standpoint and his style.[21] When a young person asks himself, "Who am I?" he is conscious of facing a great many historical alternatives and future possibilities. Man is a question-asking animal; he is also a symbol-maker—he reveals himself in what he does and how he does it. Philosophy, like theology, is also capable of "the higher or open standpoint." Philosophy, like theology, must appropriate the emergence of a thoroughgoing relativism in contemporary consciousness. Moreover, once philosophy begins to study the realities of standpoint and style, it will become very like theology; the difference between the two, on the level of the open standpoint, begins to disappear. One may study ways of life, standpoints, style, from either a theological or a philosophical starting point. Assuming an equal degree of sensitivity, fairness, and profundity, a philosopher and a theologian might be able to enter with equal success into standpoints not their own. Some day, perhaps, they may even be able to enter with equanimity into one another's standpoints. But that hope may be too sanguine—eschatological or utopian, as you wish.

V.

Radical theology quite properly has brought to our attention the collapse of the cultural context in which basic Christian symbols were once meaningful. What I have hoped to add to radical theology is the more general point that the appropriation of historical relativism by our generation makes all standpoints, not only the Christian standpoint, problematical. Secondly, I have wished to suggest that the proper methodological response to the appro-

---

[21] See Robert Jay Lifton, "Protean Man," *Partisan Review* (Winter, 1968), pp. 13–27. Lifton points out how frequently it now happens that men undergo two or more major "conversions" in one lifetime.

priation of relativism is the move to "the open standpoint": the conception of theology as a study of alternative standpoints and styles. Theology so conceived is a study of the myths, symbols, rituals, liturgies, gestures, words by which men express their individual and corporate standpoints. In our society, for example, the coffee break, the cocktail party, the seminar, the halftime marching band, the interdisciplinary conference, the telephone, the Boeing 707, black power, the Apollo rocket, *Playboy* magazine, the Mustang, counterinsurgency warfare, and other similar symbols reveal what our corporate standpoint is and show our corporate style.

In particular, the symbol "God" points to the inexhaustible drive to raise questions from which such symbols initially spring, which in their concreteness they arrest, and which when cherished uncritically they suffocate. The root of religion and radical cultural change is identical.[22] Whenever a familiar set of cultural symbols loses its cogency, the correlative image of God falls apart. Furthermore, the more thoroughly the drive to ask questions leads a man to appropriate his own relativity and to hold nothing sacred, the more thoroughly the symbol of God is, as it should be, "emptied."

> In order to arrive at having pleasure in everything.
> Desire to have pleasure in nothing.
> In order to arrive at possessing everything,
> Desire to possess nothing.
> In order to arrive at being everything,
> Desire to be nothing.
> In order to arrive at knowing everything,
> Desire to know nothing.
> In order to arrive at that wherein thou hast no pleasure,
> Thou must go by a way wherein thou hast no pleasure.
> In order to arrive at that which thou knowest not,

[22] *Belief and Unbelief,* pp. 153–154.

Thou must go by a way thou knowest not.
In order to arrive at that which thou possessest not,
Thou must go by a way that thou possessest not.
In order to arrive at that which thou art not,
Thou must go through that which thou art not.
When thy mind dwells upon anything,
Thou art ceasing to cast thyself upon the All.
For in order to pass from the all to the All,
Thou hast to deny thyself wholly in all.
And, when thou comest to possess it wholly,
Thou must possess it without desiring anything.
For, if thou wilt have anything in having all,
Thou hast not thy treasure purely in God.[23]

If it is true that God is named not in virtue of any concrete cultural creation but in virtue of the inexhaustible drive to ask questions, then that name is most accurately uttered in darkness, in silence, in negation. For any illuminating, noisy, affirmative symbol set forth in place of that name may be further questioned and its limitations exhibited.

The unrestricted drive to ask questions is like a powerful wind blowing in the night. The atheist, hearing only the silence and recognizing the negation, finds his atheism confirmed. The theist, recognizing that that negation is reached through the power of inquiry, finds in negation an underlying affirmation. Both theist and atheist, however, experience an identical darkness. Their standpoints are different. Yet it is happening more frequently nowadays that each can enter into and sympathize with the standpoint of the other, without giving up his own. That fact, in itself, seems an indication that the method here described is sound.

The new method is aptly described by a new name, as we next explore.

[23] St. John of the Cross, *ibid.,* p. 72.

11

The Trinity as Planetary Symbol

THE natural home of theology has moved from the seminary and divinity school to the university. It acquires a new name. And at the university, "religious studies" turns out to be different from "theology." For one thing, it concerns *all* the world religions.

This move from "theology" to "religious studies" occupies the inquiries of many of the bright spirits in our generation. It has unsettled many. Many Christians, even among those who claim that God is "wholly other" and that theology is as independent as possible of "culture," have discovered to how great an extent they are implicated in a refined, elaborate "cultural religion." As the supporting culture slips away, their Christian faith turns out to be a seed planted in sandy soil.

The move to "religious studies" is also casting doubt upon the enterprise of theology itself, as a *fides quaerens intellectum,* in the universe of discourse of conceptual analysis, according to academic methods. Conversations among theologians at conventions of the American Academy of Religion, at symposia, at colloquia, usually spread despair. How many professional theologians there are who no longer love their profession!

Christian theology will not perish in some homogenized soup of religious studies—unless we allow it to. Cardinal Newman once wrote that advances up the mountain require a zig-zag course: one needs elbow-room for error, for momentary descents and recapitulations, for surveys of the terrain. Three main zags are likely to be taken by Christian theology in the future.

First, many are restless with the constructions of reality imposed by what used to be called "modern consciousness," "enlightened attitudes" and "relevance." The need to conform theories of meaning and truth to criteria suitable for scientific method, "objectivity" or dominant academic philosophies is now experienced, not as liberation, but as alienation. The basic investigations must go deeper: *not* "reason and faith" but "*consciousness* and faith." Consciousness is a larger, more inclusive, more elusive domain than reason.

Secondly, where the superiority of modern, secular culture was once implicitly conceded (religion addressed "its cultured despisers"), wonder and modesty and a sense of fragility have been borne in upon almost everyone. It was important, once, to become "profane, pragmatic, and secular." It is now important to investigate the extent to which each culture, and each person, necessarily lives according to a distinctive sense of reality, set of symbols, and fund of stories.

Thirdly, no human being or culture can appropriate all actual (or possible) senses of reality, symbols, stories. Each must choose. What are the consequences of such choices for a culture or for a person? "Who are we? What shall we be?" Theological choice is forced upon us. What, then, are the implications of choosing a Christian sense of reality?

I want to offer here a fresh way of conceiving of theology, suitable for the new conditions and illuminating the past as well. Theology is, first of all, sustained and critical reflection. But it is not the kind of reflection an observer does, a scientist in a white coat. It is the reflection of a participant. It is not necessarily personal or autobiographical reflection, for a theologian must know how to enter sympathetically and critically into standpoints other than his own.

Perhaps, as a start, "articulation" is a better word than "reflection" (which has a passive, pale cast to it). Theology is sustained articulation in poor and halting words; it voices thick experience (including the experience of the Word of God), rich symbols, dense and dimly discerned stories, and encompassing, air-like senses of reality. Theology articulates. Theology interprets. Theology sees connections, exposes contradictions, becomes conscious of motifs and modalities, projects a future, recasts the past, criticizes the present.

Theology is the sustained articulation of questions of personal and communal identity. "Who am I? Who are we? How are we related to our world? Whither ought we to head?" Writing theology is not like writing physics, logic, sociology, psychology, or even anthropology. It is a little more like, but it is not, literary criticism—in that large sense which Lionel Trilling conceives and practices in *Beyond Culture*. It involves much more skill in matters of the imagination, the sensibility, and the life of culture and action than theologians trained in the skills of rational analysis tend to admit. Scorn for what one does not do well is not, however, limited to academics.

Orientation and Method

For the sake of speaking more clearly about "consciousness," we can say that every human operates from within a personal and communal standpoint. A standpoint consists of a matrix and a set of operations. The matrix is composed of five "layers": a sense of reality, a set of stories, a complex of symbols, a body of principles, a grasp of facts. The operations are also five: experiencing, imagining, understanding, judging, and doing.

The operations function within the matrix. Matrix and operations interact dynamically. The activity of one of the five operations stimulates the other operations. The operations also confirm (or unsettle) each of the five "layers" of the matrix in which they occur.

Rationalistic theology has tended to place too much attention upon two parts of the matrix (principles and facts) and one operation (understanding) to the neglect of, or even to the disparagement of, the others. Bultmann, for example, made a virtue of "demythologizing," and the words "without myth" gave promise of a purely rational illumination, as if that were commendable —or possible.

The sense of reality of the Enlightenment effectively replaced the sense of reality of Christianity; the story of progress replaced the story of the way of the cross and resurrection; and the symbols of rationalized industrial society replaced the cosmos of preindustrial towns and countryside. But even Barth erected a "biblical positivism"—different principles, different facts, same lack of awareness of the protean possibilities of consciousness on this planet.

Theology written with attention to sense of reality, story and symbol is not easily recognized for what it is. It achieves its distinctions and makes its subtle points by tone, metaphor, rhythm and voice (also in written texts) as well as by conceptual precision. It does not always *state,* although it always *shows.* Its verbs are charged with imaginative content. Its sentence structures mask unspoken secrets. It does all this because its aim is to render standpoints, not merely concepts.

Style is not separate from substance. The sloppy thinker says he will "think it out carefully," then "dress it up a little." The theological task is more like catching an experience in its textured fullness, with the images and dynamic patterns and rhythms that most exactly represent it. The substance of an insight retains a tie to the image in which it occurs, and it depends for its life upon a story and a sense of reality.

The Word of God was uttered in the Scriptures in full awareness of such dimensions as are suggested here. Sense of reality (myth), story, symbols, principles, and facts are all given due weight. Rational theology, by comparison, has often been cerebral and thin. Yet think of Augustine's dialogues, the commentaries of Aquinas, the letters of Luther, the *Thoughts* of Pascal, the many personal and "unscientific postscripts" of Kierkegaard. I do not mean that only the "existentialist" modes are to be cherished: I delight in Lonergan's "and in the thirty-seventh place," too, and in the scrupulosity of Yale theology. To each his own story; each *has* his own.

For three generations, theologians have been concerned to bring theology to "historical consciousness." Every theological word or symbol, they showed, arose at a certain point in history and had a historical function. It will be our task for another generation to bring theology to "political consciousness." The reason is not that political theology has become faddish. (As a theological maxim, "Be in fads but not of them"—a word for every season, roots elsewhere—is the condition of long fruitfulness.) We require a political theology because we have learned the extent to which social and political structures affect standpoints and are subject to manipulation.

Every theological word—faith, despair, freedom, community, identity, integrity, love, guilt, redemption—depends for its concrete significance upon the social and political context in which it is uttered. "Despair" on the part of a New Canaan housewife is concretely different from "despair" on the part of a Black mother in Loundes County.

Theology is sustained articulation. Yet its goal is not verbosity but *life:* its aim is to heal, liberate, ennoble, enrich. The lives of Americans are less and less infused by the thick, organic, historical textures of history, traditions, customs, close family ties, tribal

133

instincts. Mobility, mass media, and industrial rationalization have weakened the social textures of the past. The full weight of integrating their own lives falls more and more upon isolated individuals. Social organizations are not organic, given, necessary, but fluid and manipulatable. How, then, shall they be shaped?

That question is theological, for the context within which persons (and the culture as a whole) will actualize their identity is established by such institutions. Economic institutions relentlessly define what is to be taken as "real." Political institutions channel the forms of social action. Theology cannot be a sustained articulation of our own identity and remain neutral, naive or blind regarding institutions.

The Realities to Which We Cleave

No theory makes sense except from the standpoint within which it is conceived and verified. No "facts" are grasped as facts except within a standpoint. But a standpoint is composed of a matrix and a set of operations.

The Christian people are a historically differentiated people upon this planet, who share one or more of a large family of standpoints. There is no one Christian standpoint. There is apparently no one set of characteristics that essentially and universally, in all times and all places, distinguishes Christians from other humans. There is rather a set of senses of reality, stories, symbols, principles and facts that Christians have variously perceived and appropriated. The special place they have given the Sacred Scriptures, and the sense of being an historical people that they have nourished, have kept this matrix active in their consciousness. They have nourished the sense of being "different" and also the sense of being "universal" or "like."

134

What does it mean to share in various Christian symbols today? Consider two or three of what the ancients, wiser than we, called symbola:

(1) *"In the name of the Father, and the Son, and of the Holy Spirit."* That is to say, a *trinitarian consciousness.* An instinctive sense of reality that selects out from the vast influx of undifferentiated experience those features that build up community between persons—persons who retain their independence. Such an instinct calls those features "most real."

Reality does not come to us marked "reality." From the blooming, buzzing confusion we select—not whimsically, arbitrarily, but tutored by hard knocks—what we shall take to be real, and what we shall deem meaningless or irrelevant. To accept the Trinity as the mesh for one's sense of reality is to suppose that what is most valuable, most noteworthy, most to be enlarged in the realm of our attention and action is the building up of community.

Not just any community. "People who need people" are not the happiest people but the most draining people in the world— umbilical cords in hand, they search for sockets. We desire, rather, precisely that kind of community whose purpose is to generate in its midst independent, self-critical persons. Such persons are not stoics or "Marlboro men," but humans of independence who recognize that even their own independence is achieved only within community.

Before a community recognizes the value of personal independence in its participants, it tends to diminish its members and to limit its own growth. If it emphasizes the uniqueness, originality and independence of its members without a corresponding emphasis on the overwhelming facts of community, a community degenerates into a lonely crowd.

Three persons, wholly distinct and yet perfectly united—the Trinity—become a constitutive ideal for the participation of humans in one another's lives. On the one hand, all humans share in one same divine life; on the other, each is distinct and valuable in herself or himself. The Trinity is not exactly a model to be imitated, for the union of human beings does not reach the total identification with one another achieved by the Persons in the Trinity. But the inner life of the Trinity is participated in by humans, who accordingly are one with one another in God.

(2) "*I believe in God*." To "believe" in God is not to utter words or to affirm propositions, but to live in a certain way: namely, to cleave faithfully in one's life to the exigent dynamics of honesty in one's heart and mind; to cleave to the courage required to be honest; to cleave to that freedom without which honesty and courage are not exercised; to cleave to those bonds of community that enforce honesty, courage, and freedom as operations to be strengthened in one's life. For we need not be honest, courageous, free or communal. Promises to be so do not make us so.

No one has seen God. What God is, precisely and in blazing clarity, we do not know. Categories like "thing," "object" or even "person" take us down wrong alleys. But according to the Revelation made in Jesus, and according to our own culturally tutored experience, God is at least more like human *acts* of honesty, courage, freedom, and community than he is like anything else we know. When we experience such actions, we are more like God than in any other state we know.

As best we can discern, to participate in God's life is to live honestly, courageously, in freedom, strengthening human community. The content of the claim "I believe in God" is a set of such actions, understood as participation in a life larger than our own. In these actions, the race is one.

136

Moreover, such actions are each self-transcendent in a significant way. It is possible to say that a human who lives honestly, courageously, freely and in brotherly fashion is "merely" a man, and that there is no sign of "God" in such behavior. That is one plausible interpretation of the facts. No one sees God.

But it appears to be a mistaken interpretation. For when I am being honest, it appears that there is no part of myself that does not come under the scrutiny of such honesty. The scouring light in which my emotions, motives, insights, decisions, presuppositions, superego, instincts, and the rest come under scrutiny does not seem wholly from me. It is mine and I am responsible for it. Yet I also belong to it, and nothing in me has control over it. It seems that I am "participating" in some other.

This is especially true when, like Freud, I recover the traces of my superego by the light Freud so amply served. It is as if the "light" of honesty that operates so relentlessly and embarrassingly within me derives from a light that cannot be bribed. I am thoroughly capable of dishonesty. But in that light I am vulnerable as well to total exposure, and even in the poorly cherished honesty of my own life am step by step exposed.

The presence of courage in despair, the unavoidability of my own freedom, and the "basic trust" for whose presence in me I depend on community are in a related way signs of "transcendence" and "gift" in my life. They call us constantly beyond ourselves, beyond our present level of development. It is possible that a merely secular and agnostic or atheistic interpretation of these phenomena is acceptable. I would not wish to convert others by definition. Each human must discern her or his own identity and give it a name. To say "I believe in God" is not, therefore, either redundant or coerced, but free and significant. It is to give one's life one interpretation rather than another.

The Substance of Things Hoped For

(3) "... *and in Jesus Christ his only Son.*" The defect of liberal Protestantism and of Catholic modernism has ever been in some way to violate the scandal of concreteness, to prefer the spiritual, the enlightened and the abstract. God did not reveal himself in some blinding, universal spiritual Light but in concrete flesh in an "underdeveloped nation" in a backward, ancient age: in a finite man, Jesus. Had God appeared in some universally compelling spiritual way, outside the confines of one particular culture with its concrete horizon, stories, and symbols, perhaps all men could more directly have access to him in a unified way.

Instead, God chose the way of the concrete, of flesh, of finitude, of particularity, of fact, of *here* and *now*. Thereby we are instructed, in seeking wisdom, not to look upwards but down: at the earth, at our immediate neighbor, at our present concrete condition. We ought to regard utopias, futures, and "if only's" as forms of agnosticism and escape.

Nature and history are in tension. Jesus was born not only into natural space but into evolutionary time. Nature itself is not static but dynamic. Moreover, the logic of its development is not that of a chain of premises but that of emergent shifts in sets of probabilities—directions and contexts yield successively to new and different directions and contexts. No one logic runs through the whole. Novelty occurs. Repetition is modified.

For its part, "history" is not genuinely separable from evolutionary "nature." Man's freedom is not limitless. It is ecological. Unless humans heed certain necessities of nature, they may destroy themselves. The webs of evolutionary nature and historical freedom turn out to be one web. "The Word became flesh" is a forerunner of "history becomes evolutionary nature." Respect for the concrete, for the body, for the earth is a precondition of godliness of spirit. The urge to "master" the earth, to "transcend" the body, to seek escape from limitations of the body by way of "ecstasy" (*ekstasis*) is to misapprehend belief "in Jesus Christ, his only Son."

To believe that God manifested himself in Jesus is not to utter words, but in action to love this concrete earth, to cherish every detail of it, to recognize the epiphanies of God in the cold beads on a glass of wine, in wind in the pines on the wintry slopes, and in a dried shell on the beach. It is, moreover, to understand the urgent need for concrete ceremonies, rituals and liturgies.

Not so that these should "move" us or "do something" for us. But that we may humbly find regular occasion for concrete bodily acts in which, ordinarily without ecstasy and in silent abandonment, God is present to a small community. That is real for us which our rituals make real. Constant attendance at seminars makes talk real; constant social action makes bureaucratic or counter-bureaucratic action real. Celebration makes the mystery of unseen community real.

Thinking With the People

Jesus was born in Bethlehem, not in Manhattan. It is not, then, the publishers but the hard hats—obedient, trusting, docile ones —who were the closest matrix of his revelation. The intellectuals consider themselves an avant-garde; they show by tone and manner that they despise the ignorant and the obedient. The porters and cleaners and cooks of a seminary complex probably trust President Nixon's pledge to get us out of Vietnam and wish to support him; the avant-garde loathes both Nixon and them.

Political action for a Christian must certainly mean rootage in the people, thinking with the people, accepting the values and worldview of the people for the good and the wisdom that is in

139

them, as a precondition for criticism and leadership in some new direction. A political theology whose strength does not lie in the historical people, in all their childlikeness and complexity and anger and turmoil, is not an incarnational theology.

Dostoevsky's "gentle Christ" is no more the real Jesus than is the Grand Inquisitor. Simple people do need to be led—but by leaders who understand them from within, not by experts who show contempt and condescension for all they hold dear.

The Kingdom of God is a social and political metaphor for institutional structures in which honesty, courage, freedom and community are maximized; it is not a license for utopian hopes or a confusion of realms. The Kingdom of God begins here and now. It is not here separable from sin, corruption and irrationality. The Kingdom groans under the evils implicit in the structures of the Roman Empire, barbarian tribes, systems of slavery and the American hegemony. But it exists in every today, and it does not depend upon the "withering away" of institutions.

The Kingdom of God is not only an appeal transcending every present stage of human development, imploring that "God's will" be ever more completely done on earth until it is realized here "as in heaven." It is also the cry "Be reconciled!", the cry not to overlook the strength of that Kingdom in the present. Stronger than the forces of death, at all times, are the forces of life, even in seeming defeat. For what it means to *live* is to be honest, courageous, free, brotherly. Any other form of life— power, pragmatism, organization—is at best a means and at worst an empty, facsimile life.

Planetary Consciousness

The Christian does not expect institutions to be other than inefficient, corrupt and burdensome. But institutions are concrete, human, fallible, corporeal, heavy, resistant to spirit—and *therefore* signs for celebrating the courage of the Incarnation. God chose for us to work *through* such resistant structures, rather than in some pure, spiritual escape from them. Like yeast in heavy dough, we are called, not to escape, but to transform.

Working within, we celebrate incarnation. We also risk increasing the oppressive weight, beyond our capacity to transform it. Didn't Jesus himself help bring heavier vengeance upon his people, in all times and in all places? There is, in any case, no escape from this world and its necessities. Eschatological communities celebrate as nearly as can be done what the Kingdom "will be." Incarnational communities celebrate what it is, in its oppressive weight and in the lightening of that weight century by century until now. Our salvation both is and is not yet.

The focus of theology must increasingly be placed upon "consciousness" rather than upon "reason," for "reason" is but a thin band in the spectrum even of intelligent activity. The "reason" of science, in particular, carries with it a sense of reality, a set of stories and a set of symbols that are largely masked. Hidden, they nourish the lust to master the earth, and coldly inhibit the desire to be one with it. The urge to control appears to a Christian sense of reality both alienating and ultimately destructive. The urge to understand and to-be-one-with seems participatory and healthful.

Every human necessarily acts from a certain standpoint: within that sense of reality, telling those stories, infused by those symbols that give his actions meaning. Christians are discovering there is no one Christian standpoint, closed in advance, that establishes their own secure identity. They must, like others, in part invent and in part discover their proper identity. What it has been to be a Christian is not necessarily what it will be to be a Christian.

Still, there will be continuity with the past—not univocal, not in a straight line, but by way of the analogy of one standpoint to another. The impact of the new social and political context of post-industrial society and fresh cultural experience from the rest of the planet call forth a quantum leap in the standpoint Christions assume. But all other humans face a similar quantum leap. Christians are not alone in their confusion and newfound modesty.

From Scripture and our communal history we can derive many clues about fruitful senses of reality, stories and symbols by which to interpret our new experience. We have not been abandoned; our ancestors have not left us empty-handed. Indeed, our greatest temptation in the last 400 years appears to have crested: our temptation to accept the standpoint of the Enlightenment, its stories of progress and its symbols of Light and Darkness, Good and Evil, and to make our interpretation of Christianity function in that inhospitable context. The consequences of that standpoint, to which we turn in the next chapter, are now apparent in modern life, and almost everywhere there is a desire to reconsider.

We ought to be bold enough to speak with whatever authenticity we possess in the struggle of the human race to give cultural shape and institutional form to the senses of reality, stories, and symbols that will constitute the new planetary consciousness. A Christian standpoint will not dominate, but it may provide a conception of community that neither destroys nor exaggerates the independence of the individual person, the relation of nature to history, and a respect for the concrete. In short, the planetary consciousness might be fashioned in the image of the Trinity and the Incarnation as constitutive metaphors for the nature of man.

12

The Sudden, Sad Death of the Enlightenment

THE Enlightenment, despite its unarguable advances, was a great escape from dense human reality. Kant stated its meaning best, in answer to the question "What is Enlightenment?" The Enlightenment is consciousness: consciousness of individual autonomy. It is commitment: commitment to the procedures of universal Reason. Individuality and Mind. Will. "Enlightenment is man's leaving his self-caused immaturity. Immaturity is the incapacity to use one's intelligence without the guidance of another. . . . Have the courage to use one's own intelligence! is therefore the motto of the Enlightenment."[1] These words were written in 1784; the social situation of intelligence two centuries later makes the sentiment seem childlike.

Enlightened Reason: no more Persian myths about Light and Darkness. Progress: no more living according to mere symbols. Cocktail parties: no more communal celebrations and empty rituals. The rationalization of industry, commerce, and national life: no more heteronomy. The limits of Reason alone: no more imagination, sensuousness, mystery, incantation.

The ironies are palpable.

The dreams of Kant, Condorcet, Comte, and Mill have come too true. And of what now shall young men and women dream?

[1] New York, 1949, p. 132.

1.

As such writers as Irving Howe and Alfred Kazin have noted, growing up in the thirties was a powerful experience for the New York intellectuals.[2] Mostly of immigrant families, mostly poor, mostly Jewish, they were determined to commit themselves to an intellectual culture otherwise scarcely represented in America. They moved beyond their immigrant families—and to that extent they chose "Americanization." They moved beyond Jewish religiousness; their address to the world was resolutely secular. They felt little sympathy for the reigning American intellect—largely WASP, mainly academic, thinly historical, thickly "scientific," notably parochial. "Literary modernism" provided them with a vehicle of discourse, sensibility, and consciousness.

Irving Howe wrote in *Commentary:* "The real contribution of the New York writers was toward creating a new, and for this country almost exotic, style of work. They thought of themselves as cultural radicals even after they had begun to wonder whether there was much point in remaining political radicals. [Their contribution was] the exploration and defense of literary modernism."[3] "Political radicalism" supplied a social goal and a critical method that was more than literary.[4] For a living, some members of what Norman Podhoretz, in *Making It,*[5] refers to as "the

[2] See Alfred Kazin, *Starting Out in the Thirties,* Boston, 1965; Irving Howe, "The New York Intellectuals," *Commentary* (October, 1968), pp. 29–51.

[3] *Ibid.,* p. 34.

[4] Dwight Macdonald, *Memoirs of a Revolutionist,* New York, 1963. The New York intellectuals were less involved in issues of power, organization, or pragmatism than in ideas. Their politics were remarkably a-political, their radicalism more a religion than a politics.

[5] New York, 1969.

family" taught; others preferred the world of publishing and editing.

It is no secret—Howe roundly announces it—that today in the very moment of their cultural dominance the New York intellectuals no longer function as a family; no longer cohere; no longer have a cultural program. *Partisan Review* is not today what it was. *Commentary* is once again resolutely "making it," against the temporary dominance of *The New York Review*. Both journals have an uneasy relationship to the rest of America. Both seem to feel most comfortable when they are expressing themselves as "outsiders." Their alienation is such that the main opponent of each sometimes seems to be the other.

Who is on whose side? Who now writes where? What unsaid passions empower the spoken arguments? Why stake one's opponents out at four-points on the sand, brushing their faces with molasses? Why the grinding *ressentiment?*

The age of theology has arrived again. The issues that divide intellectuals today are no longer tame, domestic, familial. Arguments refuse to lie flat for univocal logical mapping; too many hidden meanings are carried by the terms. Disputes do not concern facts or logical procedures; horizons and standpoints are under scrutiny. The *who* of statements has become as critical as the *what*: authors write as if their psyches, their integrity, their humanity, and even their lives were at stake.

These changes are not a matter of tone but of substance. The interesting questions today are theological. Cult is the center of culture, and if (as all seem to agree) our culture is in crisis, it is in large measure because what we shall count as real, what we shall count as true, what we shall count as beautiful, what we shall count as sane, are in question. Until we decide what it is we shall defer to, emulate, and celebrate, we have no culture; we have chaos. Gods ordinarily arise out of nothingness.

145

Questions of identity are not susceptible to scientific decision. They are not merely descriptive questions. Whether the employment of scientific procedures is appropriate to, or exhaustive of, the intelligence of human beings is in part the issue.

The questions of identity are not pragmatic, either. For many aspects of our identity have little or nothing to do with "what works" for us or for anyone else. Many things we do just for the hell of it. And the *way in which* we do many things—the story we delight in living out, the bearing and significance we attach to our actions—far exceeds their efficaciousness or cash value.

Actions always carry with them an implicit sense of reality; a sense of place; a network of relations; intentionality and direction; shape and form; signature, *élan,* and style. Each action recreates in microcosm its agent's vision of self, nature, and history.

"Theological" understanding is directed toward the symbolic background of actions: what is required in order for such actions to take place, what constitutes their significance, and which criteria are involved for their evaluation. One may object that psychoanalysis, sociology, anthropology, and other disciplines are also engaged in such issues. Let us not quarrel about what name to call the necessary analysis. Attention must be drawn to the non-immediate, non-pragmatic, non-scientific dimensions of human action; let us attend to them by any method available to us.

2.

Since at least the thirteenth century, faith and reason—or philosophy and theology—have been deemed to be separate and different from one another. Fundamental shifts in our culture have now made such a distinction untenable. On the one hand,

146

theologians can no longer work merely within the confines of "revelation," a religious tradition, or a denominational orthodoxy. Wholly unprecedented questions have been raised for them, concerning the location of the individual in the social system, the interpretation of world cultures and religions, ecumenism, technology, and vastly increased knowledge in virtually every field. When theologians address themselves to such questions, as they must, they are thrown back upon the same native intelligence and secular conceptual equipment as everybody else. Inexorably, they sound more and more like humanists or philosophers.

On the other hand, philosophers can no longer work merely within the confines of "reason," let alone "logic," or even "language." Belief in "pure reason" does not meet the tests of practice. Not only primitives (Levi-Strauss) but all men "think with their stomachs." One cannot adequately distinguish "the cognitive" from the "emotive"—the very impulse to do so is suspect. The more concretely a philosopher inquires into the constituents of human action, the more he is drawn away from models based upon mechanics, mathematics, and the language and laws of the natural sciences. He has to begin to take account of the imaginations of agents (not least, philosophers), the struggles in which they believe their actions to be engaged, the signals by which they distinguish allies from enemies, the stories they believe themselves to be living out, the rituals by which they renew themselves, rededicate themselves, and announce in concentrated reënactment what it is they are doing. The more concretely a philosopher thinks about the way human beings actually act, the more "theological" his perceptions tend to become.

Pluralism on a worldwide scale teaches us that there are a multiplicity of identities which men may today fashion for themselves. The language of presuppositions, axioms, principles, beliefs is far too narrowly rational to explain how men (not least of all, rationalists) in fact act. Each man has his own vision, imagination, sensibility, direction, and determination—a standpoint peculiar to himself. Insofar as we study standpoints, we perform analyses that are larger and more complex than either theology or philosophy enabled us to perform in the past. The inner lives and the actions of men today are more complex than in earlier societies. The sources of their imaginations, passions, aspirations, and senses of reality are more various than was common among men in the past. Men today, in "advanced" nations at least, participate in many cultural traditions at once.

Philosophy and theology, we've seen, can no longer be adequately distinguished from one another. Each man chooses a sense of reality, stories, symbols, according to which, in the context of which, and according to the criteria of which, he perceives, imagines, thinks, judges, acts. To untangle that skein, the student of human action can ill afford to limit himself "within the bounds of reason alone," *or* within the bounds of a single theological orthodoxy. Both "reason" and "orthodoxy" are powerless to institutionalize (and simplify) what men take to be real. To be intelligent today a man necesarily draws nourishment from many diffuse and separate sources. His sensitivities and imagination must be freer and more alert than the cult of "pure reason" led our forefathers to propose. Questions must be faced that no orthodox symbols or traditions wholly prepare him to assimilate.

3.

Not long ago, Harry Levin published an essay, "What Was Modernism?" The poignancy of the past tense is appropriate. Lionel Trilling's answer to the question "What is the modern element in modern literature?" was succinct: an anti-cultural or counter-cultural bias. Richard Ellmann and Charles Feidelson add: "Committed to everything in human experience that militates against custom, abstract order, and even reason itself, modern literature has elevated individual existence over social man, unconscious feeling over self-conscious perception, passion and will over intellection and systematic morals, dynamic vision over the static image, dense actuality over practical reality. In these and other ways, it has made the most of its break with the past, its inborn challenge to established culture."[6]

"Modernist literature," Irving Howe tells us in the introduction to yet another anthology,[7] "is coming to an end . . . what awaits it is . . . the kind of savage parody which may indeed be the only fate worse than death."

Is today's "counter culture" the "savage parody" of the literary modernism we assimilated these last forty years? What those who made common cause with literary modernism had in mind, while introducing it into an initially unresponsive, adolescent, optimistic, and relentlessly progressive America, was not an *end* to culture. What they had in mind was the establishing of culture —the building up, in America, of critical intelligence, the discernment of diffuse and difficult sensibilities, discrimination, a delicate perception of nuance, the enthronement of mind and reason and measure. We witness everywhere the "radicalization" of modernists, and their "de-radicalization," while they make up their minds how they stand vis-à-vis the counter culture. Did the neo-modernists, the young, take as the theme what their elders meant only as counterpoint?

I am not yet willing to affirm that the counter culture is a direct descendant of literary modernism. Irving Howe, in a not

[6] "Preface," *The Modern Tradition,* New York, 1965, p. vi.
[7] *Literary Modernism,* Greenwich, 1967, pp. 13–40.

quite convincing passage, suggests three or four major differences between the outlook of modernism and the outlook of the New Left.[8] What I want to assert is that an hiatus has occurred in American intellectual culture. Literary modernism seems to have crested, and in its recession its defenders, apologists, and chroniclers appear to be embarrassed. Unless I am mistaken, the whole enterprise of "the humanities" is, for this and other reasons, in critical and fundamental disarray. What *is* "Western culture"? And what about all those other cultures?

4.

A related embarrassment seems to affect the social sciences. A conjunction of favorable stars gave the social sciences a sudden intellectual preëminence in the decade just past; and those stars have begun to separate. As never before in history, the individual in trying to establish his personal (and even social) identity could not rely upon cultural, economic, social, political, and religious institutions to tell him solidly and securely what is real, true, good, beautiful. So fragmented, so pluralistic, so mobile, and so complexly structured is advanced industrial society that the full crushing weight of establishing his own "reality" falls upon each solitary individual. *Whether* he fashions for himself an integrated identity, and *how* he will do so, is left to his "consumer preference." The individual, as never before, is atomic.[9]

The social scientist aspiring to "creative engineering" appears to have an unparalleled opportunity. Few are the residual, social cohesions tying individuals into firm, resistant social groups;

[8] "The New York Intellectuals," *op. cit.,* pp. 47 f.

[9] Thomas Luckmann, *The Invisible Religion,* New York, 1967, pp. 98–106.

few are the thick, tangled roots of connections to the past. In-dividuals are extraordinarily vulnerable to rearrangement and realignment. The bias of scientific method leads its practitioners to discount precisely those intangible, mythic cohesions, tradi-tions, and legitimations which now appear at their historical weakest. The social scientists (not the best of them but those of ordinary cut) have been free to test "opinion" and to scant "conviction." On the one hand, the rationalistic bias prefers opinions; on the other, convictions—those passional, traditional, death-defying commitments whose roots lie obscured in history and the social psyche—seem nowadays to be so weak.

The embarrassment of the social sciences today arises from the theological dimension which is implicit in any and every scheme to reform or to revolutionize a society. *Who are we?* What sort of society do we wish to construct? Granted that we can re-build all the cities on the face of this planet, what sort of cities ought we to build? What in the development of humans ought we to encourage? What in them ought we to inhibit? It is not, furthermore, certain that the manipulation of social institutions —by whom?—is compatible with the untrammeled freedom of the individual psyche. Is our ideal a radical *laissez-faire,* a radical "do your thing"? Or is it a communal enterprise of building up mutual concern, mutual support, mutual labor upon mutual projects? Optimal relations between social conditioning and personal liberty, and between the individual, the community, and the social order, have not been discerned—nor can they be—scientifically.

If the social scientist is merely a describer of what happens, he appears to be "in complicity." If he prescribes what should be, he appears to be prophet, king, and priest. If he merely describes, calculates, and predicts probable consequences of alternative courses of action, he appears to pretend to more knowledge than the state of his science seems to warrant: face to face with racial hatreds and ethnic animosities, he appears innocent.

The natural scientist, as well, wears no more clothes today than any other intellectual. Just yesterday, any young man who donned the pure white chasuble of the laboratory and performed his tasks with devotion and an ardent ritual accuracy could feel duly reassured that his every action furthered human "progress." Every step he took advanced the race's "enlightenment." Every clarification he achieved banished by so much the hereditary darkness. Just yesterday, no one suggested that each step forward in scientific concentration might be—*might* be—leading the human race one step closer to annihilation. Just yesterday, nobody believed that scientific knowledge, whether in itself or in its use, was efficacious more for the destruction than for the enhancement of this planet. It is not so certain today that the young person who wishes to give his or her life to human survival and human development should enter upon a career in chemistry, physics, biology, or research medicine. That faith is nourished and propagandized by some; its churches, too, are beginning to empty.

5.

What, then, shall we do? Begin a new religion? That task is far more difficult than many imagine. Religions—even science, even atheism—are not primarily matters of the head. One does not produce them as one produces a pollution-free automobile, on demand. A religion is not a problem to be solved, not a means to some other end. A religion is—all of these at once, on every human level at once—an experience, an image, a conception, a sense of reality, a dynamism of decision and action heading in a given direction, a reconciliation, a source of joy and betrayal and peace and guilt, a transcendent background such as History or Science or Progress, if not Providence, supply. It is the sense of place, meaning, and purpose that, for example, science, art, or revolution confer on those who make them a way of life.

It is important to stress that when Americans say the word "religion" they tend to have in mind something far more narrow than the word, in this context, is intended to convey. They think of Cardinal Spellman, Billy Graham, Norman Vincent Peale, ministers at weddings, funerals, and state occasions; of suburban churches, and denominational magazines. The term "religion" is wider, however, than the term "ecclesiastical" or "churchy." It means something quite different from social organizations, creeds, worship services, or even belief in God. It is synonymous, rather, with "way of life." It is a one-word equivalent for the standpoint, images, purposes, and criteria of judgment according to which an individual (or a culture) shapes world and self. It is legitimate, then, to speak of atheistic religions (like Buddhism, or that "invisible religion" of the industrialized countries of which Thomas Luckman has written).

In this sense, the Enlightenment itself was a religion, or cluster of religions. It gave rise to a new way of life. It was far more pervasive in individual and cultural behavior than a new set of intellectual beliefs. It altered the sense of reality, stories, and symbols of men as well.

A religion is, first of all, a selection. Human beings are neither infinite nor immortal. They cannot do everything at once. Our culture cannot do everything that every other culture in the past has done or today is doing. Every decision taken, each institution formed, each word newly minted gives definition. America cannot be all things to all men. God himself, becoming man, becomes *this* man in *this* place, and cannot become all human possibilities to the satisfaction of all: even *were* America God's

153

country, it could not become the one form for all men on this planet.

Civilization necessarily generates its discontents. The word is shabbily used today, but there is, and can be, no "non-repressive" society. The extravagant value placed upon the satisfaction of the individual psyche in typical American fantasies is no sign of its proponents' intelligence, experience, or self-perception. The most acute personal satisfactions are seldom solitary. They are nearly always communal in origin, structure, and significance, even when they occur in solitude. Man *is* a social animal. Presumably, then, it is both natural to him, and inevitable, that he bear with discontentment. It may even be a mark of an individual's humanity if he bears his own discontent cheerfully enough not to mupltiply the discontent of others.

I stress this point only to throw what little weight I have against an insanity fast growing in this troubled nation: that each individual's instant satisfaction of every felt "need" is a contribution to social revolution. Agree for a moment that our society is "sick"—the most advanced symptoms tend to appear more and more among intellectuals, on the left, in the youth culture, and on our college and university campuses. The implausibility of the desire for a "non-repressive" society, where each individual pleasantly "does his thing," so staggers the imagination that one hardly knows how to oppose it.

The main point, however, is that disputation over fundamental claims about the nature of the human person, the nature of society, the nature of nature, and the nature of history is what characterizes intellectual life in America today. What *is* a humane way of life today? "Who are we? What ought we to do? What may we hope?"

Such questions are not "merely" intellectual. Political leaders the world over sense the vast restlessness of their peoples. The

Machiavellian and self-serving leader must try to imagine whither this restlessness may lead in the next five years or next decade, lest it pass him by, tumble him from power, overwhelm him. Not often in history do intellectual and political questions so thoroughly intersect.

One conclusion to be drawn is that a gap between intellectuals and people, if it appears, is intellectually, politically, and culturally disastrous. A religion invented by intellectuals for intellectuals will have no roots; it will not be a cult that could be the center either of a culture or of a political movement. A religion invented out of mental exercise will almost certainly have the smell of paper flowers. A way of life arises out of shattering experiences—experiences which shatter an accepted sense of reality and cry out for a new one. There has been no lack of such experiences in our century. What we lack is the knack of interpretation: the genius, perhaps, to *allow* ourselves to be genuinely shattered and to find the new form which expresses our new identity.

6.

Two reasons help explain our failure. The first arises from the social situation of the middle-class intellectual. Whether in the academic or the publishing world, he has economic and moral security. On the other hand, his preferred self-image is that of alienation: he has contempt for the "American way of life," in its business culture and in its ethnic cultures. America both rewards him adequately and is not readily converted to his way of life. It would be much more gratifying to be poor while holding power over the spirit.

Secondly, the tradition in which intellectuals ordinarily define themselves is that of the Enlightenment. Those who pursue the ways of Reason are "enlightened"; those who do not are not. "Each individual should make up his own mind." "Each individual should develop his or her own individuality." "Each person is the equal of every other." "Each person should do whatever he decides to do, as long as it causes no harm to others."

To the emphasis on Reason which one side of the Enlightenment encourages, the other and more Romantic side, developed most fully in the tradition of literary modernism, counterposes an emphasis on need, instinct, and will. "Needs should be satisfied, instincts expressed, will given rein."

Such moral imperatives are, first of all, enormously supportive of the status quo. They rationalize quite well the fragmentation, alienation, and consumerdom of advanced industrial society. The "enlightened" have established the legitimacy of that sense of reality generated by scientific method and its technological elaboration. "Thirty years ago, when I began to write," Van Wyck Brooks said at Hunter College in 1941, "the future was an exciting and hopeful vista. Everyone believed in evolution as a natural social process. We took the end for granted. Mankind was marching forward." He attached the rising pessimism.

Defending modernism against Brooks, Dwight Macdonald drew attention to "the overmastering reality of our age: the decomposition of the bourgeois synthesis in all fields."[10] Yet it was always something of an embarrassment to the upholders of the modernist tradition that so many of their major figures— Joyce, Eliot, Proust, Pound, Ortega y Gasset—were politically reactionary.

On the one hand, many of the enlightened championed a radical utopian politics quite out of the reach of American or any other concrete society. ". . . I remember once walking in the street and suddenly really seeing the big heavy buildings in their

[10] *Op. cit.,* p. 208.

156

obstinate actuality and realizing I simply couldn't imagine all this recalcitrant matter transformed by socialism. How would the street look when the workers took it over, how would, how could revolution transfigure the miles and miles of stubborn stone? I couldn't conceive of a flame hot enough to melt into new forms this vast solid Is," Dwight Macdonald recalled years later.[11] On the other hand, values the enlightened ones espoused served quite well to legitimize the society we have. They attacked the American way of life; they also reinforced its individualism, its laissez-faire, its easy utopianism, its lack of a tragic sense, its mobility and thorough rationalization, its lack of roots, tradition, cohesiveness, connectedness. They were themselves mirror images of the society they hated. More lonely than saints among sinners, they came to hate the unenlightened, who were so much like them. The root of a certain contempt for the American way of life seems often to have been self-hatred.

What stands most in the way of an adequate contemporary religion is the dominant religion: the religion of Enlightenment, its clergy the avant-garde, its pagans middle Americans. Much is written about anti-intellectualism in America, not quite so much about the contempt intellectuals have for Rotarians, rednecks, truck drivers, and churchgoers. The hatred on both sides is theological. They trumpet mutually incompatible images of man's humanity.

Let us imagine for a moment an ecumenical movement between professors and the husbands of the motherly secretaries at their universities, between New York publishers and truck drivers. The chasm in sense of reality and sensibility is rather vast. Are all the beauties and virtues on one side? Who are the "more advanced" types? In what respects?

[11] *Ibid.,* pp. 4–5.

It is possible that there is no enduring ground between persons whose intelligence, imagination, sensibilities, and attitudes have been formed in divergent ways. Comrades in World War II, apparently, achieved a rapport which was later to vanish. Perhaps America is and must be a nation of at least two cultures which cannot interpenetrate.

"The United States," Henry Mencken wrote from one side, "is essentially a commonwealth of third-rate men . . . distinction is easy here because the level of culture, of information, of taste and judgment, of ordinary competence is so low."[12] John W. Aldridge sounds the echoing note: "A surprising number of the writers and intellectuals of the twenties and thirties—and even a few who reached maturity in the forties—had grown up in the small towns of the Middle West and South and early suffered the trauma of estrangement from a provincial culture which either had no interest in artistic and intellectual values or was actively hostile to them. . . . [These intellectuals] remembered having personally and traumatically confronted in the real Winesburgs, Zeniths, and Gopher Prairies in which they grew up—the hostility to culture, the emotional impoverishment, the moral hypocrisy, the Babbittry and Boosterism, the emptiness or ugliness of the physical surroundings, the absence of civilized amenities . . . modern America is physically a proletarian world and the perfect embodiment of the philosophy that we were put on earth to work hard and not to live well. Our physical environment was created to meet the material needs of large masses of people who were either laboring men or who shared the tastes of laboring men. Hence life in this country imposes no aesthetic hardship on that part of the population who, regardless of how well edu-

[12] "On Being An American," *Prejudices: A Selection,* James T. Farrell, editor, New York, 1955, p. 98.

cated they may be in a formal way, have the sensory equipment of peasants or early learned how to look at their surroundings without seeing them. But for the person quirky enough to be environmentally sensitive, life here can be a nightmare from which he is much too awake to awaken, an experience of visual trauma so profound that life on the moon would seem a godsend to him, if only because it would be merely bleak. He is obliged to exist in a society formed physically on values radically opposed to his own, and constantly erosive of his own . . . [American society is] a serious obstacle to the pursuit of the civilized life."[13]

Perhaps our task in the United States is not primarily that of inventing a new religion, but that of inventing a culture in which all can share. We cannot do that if the "enlightened" despise "those of peasant taste," and if common people reciprocate.

Great religions have ordinarily been founded by men whose wisdom spoke to cultivated and uncultivated alike. Is there no shared wisdom between the enlightened and the middle Americans, the yahoos and the avant-garde? Many educated persons seem to have empathy for the blacks, the Chicanos, and the Indians; it might not be impossible for them to come to recognize those respects in which Polish mill workers, Italian cab drivers, Greek barbers, and Slavic truck drivers live lives superior to their own.

It might be fun to discover America, not through the elitist lenses required by the myth of the avant-garde, and not through the egalitarian lenses required by the myth of the revolutionary vanguard, but simply through the lenses by which one clear-eyed person faces another: separate, unequal, unlike, but respectful,

[13] *In the Country of the Young,* New York, 1970, pp. 44, 46, 34, 31–32.

willing to learn, and responsive. There is no need to give in to the American temptation to put other people down.

Such mutuality might be something less than a religion. But the weight of fairly representative religious traditions would be behind it. It would go far toward creating a civil conversation in America. That is not the least prerequisite of any civilization, let alone religion, in which most of us would care to participate.

For a Catholic, the relationship of intellectuals to people is not that of "enlightened" to "unenlightened." God lives in the latter as well as in the former. In the humblest often lie hidden his choicest revelations. The task of intellectuals is to *find words for* the anguish and the aspirations of the people—not to "enlighten" but "to give tongue to." They are not a voice *to* the people, but a voice *of* the people: *vox populi,* not *avant-garde.* It is in giving voice that they lead. In a sense, therefore, they first must follow.

So many of the "unenlightened" are Catholics: our people, our own as we are theirs. Our responsibilities, like theirs, are political as well as theological: to build a world of civil conservation in which the humblest are not excluded.

13

From Belief to Politics

How does belief in God bring us to politics?

An axiom of political theology: Every theological utterance is understood within a socio-political matrix. The theologian who does not decipher the socio-political bearing of theological utterances does not account for their full significance.

The problem of God is in part a problem of a new, powerful religion which has superseded Christianity; and it is in part a problem of politics. It is a problem of experience rather than a problem of theory.

It is not true that action, in all respects, precedes theory (*actio sequitur esse*); but in some respects it does. On the one hand, before we begin to theorize we have already been acting for many years, and we have already absorbed into our tissue the socio-political project of the culture to which we belong. In this sense, we are in action long before we begin to theorize, and our theories acquire a context from the praxis of which they are a part.[1]

On the other hand, fidelity to the drive to understand leads us to that dark night beneath the depths of our culture, beneath the depths of our own instinctive actions.[2] Fidelity to understand-

---

[1] I have elaborated this point in a criticism of Lonergan which *Commonweal* entitled "The Lonergan Explosion" (May 29, 1970), pp. 268–270, and in the paper (unpublished) I presented at the Lonergan Conference (April, 1970) entitled "The Political Theology of Bernard Lonergan."

[2] Further elaborated in my *The Experience of Nothingness*, New York, 1970.

ing—through theory and imagination—may precede action and lead in fact to dramatic breakthroughs in the future possibilities of action. In this sense, reflection often precedes and liberates action.[3]

In some ways, then, action is first; in others, theory is first. The conflict between theory and action is often first felt among youth, who are trying to learn the signals concerning how they should live.

1. The Invisible Religion

When those on the left use the word "youth," they are commonly thinking of the astonishing outburst of radical politics among college youth in elite colleges during the late 1960's. There is good reason for singling out youthful elites, whose contribution to leadership in the future may be presumed to be unusually significant. But the social bias involved must not be overlooked. Among voters between 21 and 30 in the presidential election of 1968, for example, a higher percentage than in other age groups did not vote; and among those who did, George Wallace found greater support than in any other age group.[4] California is a pacesetter for the nation's youth, and there are signs that in 1971 electoral politics is decidedly "in" again, and that high school students are enrolling overwhelmingly—from 3 to 1 to 90 to 1—as Democrats.[5] But the main point to be stressed is that the word "youth" demands some care. Which youth? Where? In what socio-political context?

[3] This side of the issue is overlooked by activists and organizers, as for example Jerry Rubin in Do It!, New York, 1970.

[4] Scammon and Wattenberg, The Real Majority, New York, 1970, pp. 46–53.

[5] Steven V. Roberts, "Youths on Coast Swell Voter List," New York Times, May 23, 1971.

Peter Berger pointed out in *Movement and Revolution*[6] that one must distinguish youth culture, the movement, and radical politics. Of these, by far the narrowest circle is the last. Many who consider themselves part of "the movement"—for peace, for ecology, for social change—are by no means radical in their politics. The largest circle by far, however, is that of youth culture—those millions of young people, especially those in college, whom a number of contemporary pressures continue to separate for a long time from the acculturation of adulthood. They are too old to maintain the affectionate home life of their childhood; too young to have to accept the impersonality and compromises of bureaucratic life. They blow back and forth like the leaves of Dante's Limbo.

For economic necessity and economic affluence have created a new institutionless world in which many young people are thrown for the period of their twenties. There is no need of them in the labor force and the general affluence so far guarantees that they will not starve. Their parents no doubt showed more respect for their individuality, and treated them more reasonably, than any parents in the history of the race. Vice-President Agnew refers to this change in the dignity accorded children as "permissiveness." But there is evidence that the causes are structural and economic as well as psychological. Hence, as the industrial revolution and the enlightenment discovered childhood, and as the period during and after World War II discovered teenagers, so now technetronic societies have invented twentyhood.

It used to be that young men of sixteen or eighteen were thrown a spear or a shovel and told to go to work; and they commonly took wives and soon had children whose lives were dependent on their skills. Today, sexual experience is through

[6] With Richard Neuhaus, New York, 1969. See also my *Politics: Realism and Imagination,* New York, 1971, pp. 140–62.

technology readily available apart from marriage; and young men of the middle class are economically marginal. Past determinants of maturity, therefore, are no longer at work. Many young people at twenty find themselves thoroughly dispensable—at least as dispensable as used cars, houses, neighborhoods, landmarks, whole sections of cities. They are brought up, moreover, in the most atomic and lonely of societies in human history.[7]

I am speaking, of course, of middle-class young people, among whom readers of books are most likely to work. I am speaking not so much of the most ideologically informed, but of that great majority who have not yet come to political, ideological consciousness. Indirectly, what I say bears on the poor, the black, and even on the lower-middle-class white who does not go to college; but my main focus is on the white middle-class college population.[8]

Nearly all young people today feel a great insecurity, a sense of transience, a feeling of homelessness.[9] In every social class, there is a feeling of "things coming apart," of uncertainty, anger, and hostility. For the upper middle class in elite schools, especially, no profession seems pure, noble, humane; every avenue into the future seems either tainted, or blocked, or threatened. Should a young person become a lawyer, a doctor, a scientist, a clergyman, a worker, a soldier, a politician? Whichever way a young person turns there are influential others who accuse him (her) of "selling out," of contributing to the problem rather than to the solution; there is little sense of dignity, or security, or inner peace, and much self-doubt. Youth is classically a time of

[7] Philip Slater, *The Pursuit of Loneliness,* Boston, 1970.

[8] See Peter L. and Brigitte Berger, "The Blueing of America," *The New Republic* (April 3, 1971), pp. 20–23.

[9] Robert Bellah, 1970 Dudleian Lecture at Harvard, "No Direction Home" (unpublished).

uncertainty. But twentyhood is prolonged uncertainty, and it occurs today in the midst of vast cultural uncertainties as well.

The dominant religion in America, meanwhile, is not Christianity. It is, rather, and at its best, the "civil religion," the religion of the "American way of life," of which Robert Bellah has written.[10] It is, at its worst, the "invisible religion" of which Thomas Luckmann has written.[11] The characteristics of this dominant religion bear upon young people in an especially grinding way.

The invisible religion of America is a pervasive pragmatism and a thorough ordering of life. As much as possible, the sacred is driven out. What Harvey Cox once called "the profane, the pragmatic, and the secular" nearly fills the background consciousness of young people at suburban and urban high schools. On the one hand, cars, peers, money, activities, television, movies, music mark their faces with a certain hardness. On the other hand, many have been deeply affected by the gentleness and softness symbolized by Woodstock. Their childhood world was highly relational, at least in the limited sphere of the small family.

Many of the young grow up to an astonishing degree apart from contact with adults. Many suffer from suburban deprivation. Essentially, most know asphalt streets, lawns, automobiles; few know woods, fields, farmwork, mountains, sea. The adults from whom they might learn human motivations and angularity are their parents; a few of their parents' friends, glimpsed casually; their busy teachers; and television characters—few have lived in extended families or tightly knit neighborhoods. Most know little of hunger, disease, hardship, death, agony or other disasters which have been the common inheritance of most of

[10] *Beyond Belief,* New York, 1970, pp. 168–189.
[11] *The Invisible Religion,* New York, 1967.

mankind. Thus they scarcely know a world in which wisdom is wrested from pain, a world in need of crucifixion and redemption, a world of profound tragedy. The middle-class young are in some respects remarkably innocent; in others, far more experienced than their parents were at a comparable age.

According to the invisible religion, especially as it is lived and taught by the Americanized middle classes, slow but steady progress is always being made. Life is inherently reasonable. Humans are fundamentally good. Failures or betrayals result because somebody "blew it." (They had it made, and they blew it.) The interior life of participants in the invisible religion is flattened down—little of the orneriness, stubbornness, eccentricity, angularity, passion, or madness of those of our grandparents or uncles who came from "the old country." Their descendants are smoother, more tolerant, hang loose, play things by ear, learn early not to be obdurate or obstinate, learn how to be liked. Until the advent of "the crazies," those among them voted by their schoolmates as "having the most personality" would in other generations in other places been thought to be exactly the persons of *no* personality. They smile a lot. Like Miss America, television personalities, and successful politicians.

The invisible religion in America hangs around all of us like the invisible gas of which Bernanos wrote in *The Diary of a Country Priest;* tasteless, colorless, it seeps into our lungs; or settles on our shoulders like ash. Although a great many young Americans contemplate suicide, although excruciating loneliness is designed into the structure of our lives, although pervasive neuroses and uncertainties are everywhere manifest, the invisible religion insists that life is rational, that things will get better, that it is our patriotic duty to love our land or leave it—and that one must not talk about the underground impulses, madnesses, and evil secrets of the heart. No one in high school does. It is not

166

the wise, the good, the American thing to do. There is often great rage just under the surface of the skin.

Meanwhile, Americans long to maintain that the intimate group to which they belong is fundamentally good, decent, and humane. Evils are projected outwards upon others of evil will. *Others* are the source of evil. "The system," or "outside agitators."

A fundamental instinct of life in America is pathos. The category "victim" is a favorite self-image. The classical political emotion of the Protestant bourgeoisie dominates discussion: moral indignation. In most situations, the conservative is indignant at troublemakers; the liberal is indignant at extremists; the radical is indignant at corruption. The inmost secret of the pathetic way of life is the category "victim": *I,* who am good, *have been wronged! I,* poor racist, imperialist, fascist, male chauvinist, *am so terribly sorry![12]* The most American characteristic is to indulge in feelings of guilt, and to manipulate others through guilt. We are a nation of preachers. A tragic sense would lead us to expect less of ourselves. The pathetic sense leads us to a novel *delectatio morosa:* "Tell me again how guilty I am." "Make me feel guilty again."

What does it mean for immigrants to "become Americanized"? In part, it means to be shaped to the demands of the invisible religion. The motifs are vaguely related to Christian motifs, especially to motifs of Protestant Christianity. It is important to see—with more nuances than there is time to linger upon—that such Americanization afflicts some Americans of all social classes and all political persuasions. The invisible

[12] An example from Harvey Cox: "As a male and probably as a chauvinist (though I'm working on it), I was shaken and awakened. . . ," his review of *The Follies,* "The Cultural Captivity of Women," *Christianity and Crisis* (May 31, 1971), p. 112. Guilt can be a fruitful emotion; also destructive.

167

religion is not the property of "middle America" or of "the silent majority." It unites conservatives, liberals and radicals alike in a great national liturgy. Each is the indispensable demon for the others. The fundamental belief of each is that when the others are at last converted and become like them—or at least when their side *wins*—the sun will rise behind the peaceful hills.

The difficulty the invisible religion makes for the problem of God is pervasive and fundamental. In the invisible religion, there is little room for experiences that are not rational, ordered, and instrumentalist. In the large organizations to which Americans necessarily belong, people frequently feel "used." Emotions are a threat to objectivity. Upward mobility entails constantly shifting priorities and values. Technology and advertising make everything dispensable. We *say,* of course, that each human person has an inalienable dignity. Yet there are almost no visible signs, no ceremonies, no rituals in which the everlasting, permanent, and indestructible dignity of persons is celebrated. Instead, everything we touch is marked for obsolescence, discarded, replaced. The average American friendship, according to a major women's magazine, lasts 2½ years. People move away from one another. Friends are dispersed across the city or the nation. Transience is our style. "Freedom," according to an astute observer in *Psychology Today,* the *Stimmen der Zeit* of the invisible religion, is now defined as "the ability to move."[13] Durkheim saw the periodization of history as nomadic, agrarian, and industrial; and now we have become nomads again.

The consequence is a vast internal emptiness. There is no home. There is no "sky god." The time of confidence, direction, clear imperatives dissolves into a time of vulnerability, wandering, and rage. In the vacuum it is not the mother goddess Earth,

[13] Eugene Jennings, "Mobicentric Man," July 1970, pp. 35–36, 70, 72.

really, who wins allegiance; nor even the temple prostitutes, whose task was, like a sensitivity session or T-group, to arouse deadened feelings in order that religion might again become possible. Baal calls. "Freedom now!" Life is precious and short. Hence the demand for a non-repressive society. "Keep your motherfucking hands off me! Let me *live!*"[14] "Power to the people!" "All power to the imagination!" Or, on the other side: "The great mass of law-abiding decent people out there know the power of one four-letter word: VOTE!" "Law and order."

Abyss cries out to abyss. The heavily structured public society, and the intensely individual private society. The invisible religion depends upon a heavily organized, disciplined bureaucracy and yet extols the right of each individual to do whatever he damn well pleases.[15] The nation comes apart.

2. The Political Dilemma

The invisible religion is the Anglo-Saxon way of life as it has developed in America: the cult of the individual, together with the cult of objective technique. Both of these cults are hostile to the sense of community on which Christianity depends. Among many, the impact of the invisible religion is indifference to Christianity. The experiences in which Christianity might take root do not occur. The soil is too thin.

Among others, contempt for the invisible religion generates well-worn[16] responses. The classical American response to over-

[14] See the most revealing interview with David Harris in *American Report,* April 30, 1971.

[15] See Marshall Berman's extraordinary study of radical individualism, *The Politics of Authenticity,* New York, 1970.

[16] On reflection, it occurs to me that "groovy" may be a metaphor deriving from the fit of a needle to the track of a long-playing record: a delicate fit, a touch "in tune with" its receiver.

organization is a revival movement based on the cult of immediate experience. When the cities become effete, go west, young man! Seek the land without fences. But immediate experience leads to sectarian fracturing; and the sects oscillate between a-political and highly political religious feeling. Such a pattern is once again being played out today.

Pentecostalism, the "Jesus freaks," the human potential movement, ecology, dropping out, and radical politics—in each of these the importance of awakening primal experience is high. Each takes the form of invoking a new awareness, a conversion to a new way of perceiving reality, and a salvation. Each offers salvation both to self and to the culture. *The Greening of America,* like *The Secular City,* like *Uncle Tom's Cabin,* is not so much an argument or a theory; it is a tract. Its fundamental appeal is not that one should argue with it sentence by sentence, but that one should become converted and live. To fasten on single propositions is to be uptight; acquire a new consciousness first, and then state the propositions better if you can.

For religious studies the present turmoil opens fruitful possibilities.[17] We live during a rare conjunction of favorable stars. The chief theological arguments of our time are, in their consequences, acutely political. The chief political arguments of our time are, in their depth and form, theological problems. What shall we become? For what vision shall we give our efforts and our lives? What does it mean to be humane, authentic, fully human, under conditions of cultural and social turmoil?

To avoid political judgment today is to speak of God only in the abstract, remotely, without seeming to be in touch with reality. It is to speak of an unreal God. On the other hand, to

[17] The scope of religious studies is specified in my *Ascent of the Mountain, Flight of the Dove,* New York, 1971.

talk about God in the teeth of such winds is to struggle like Demosthenes with pebbles in his mouth beside the sea: excellent practice.

Let me, then, cut quickly through comments that might be made about the various revivalist movements named above. The deepest argument cuts as follows: Does believing in God entail joining a revolutionary movement? That is a fundamental way of grasping what is wrong with the invisible religion.

To believe in God is not to say "I believe in God." As far as the grammar is concerned, anyone can say those words. Is the test, then, to say them and to *feel* them? But feelings are notoriously deceptive. To feel them in a certain way, during prayer perhaps? But prayer, too, is notoriously various: there are good prayers and inauthentic prayers. How does anyone *know* that he believes in God, and is not deceiving himself?

The problem of God is not fundamentally a problem about how to speak; it is fundamentally a problem of how to live.[18] We can easily conceive of persons "believing in God" who never even utter the word "God," and of others who feel something mysterious, comforting or terrifying when they do so—both nevertheless being in bad faith. Not everyone who says "Lord, Lord!"—we have it on good authority—enters the kingdom of heaven.[19]

St. John's first letter is remarkably succinct. What does it mean, he asks, to believe in Jesus Christ? You must live as Jesus lived. The man who says he loves God but hates his neighbor is a liar, and the truth is not in him. To believe in God is not to say

---

[18] This point is enlarged in my "Newman on Nicaea," *Theological Studies* 21 (1960), pp. 444–453 and "The Christian Intellectual—According to Origen," *Spiritual Life* (1969), pp. 279–291.

[19] See my *Belief and Unbelief,* New York, 1965.

words but to act; it is to act, precisely, for one's fellow man.[20] And what, today, are the acts needed by our fellow men?

The demands of humans are for the first time in history planetary. The voices of poverty and brokenness and injustice come to our ears from every continent. To believe in God today is to act effectively in response to those voices. We are called so to act, not out of charity but out of justice. The issue is not aid; the issue is an equitable distribution of the fruits of the earth.[21] It is a theological maxim of the first importance that the goods of the earth are not owned by any human. They can be held in stewardship, they cannot be possessed.[22] The goods of the earth belong, properly *to the human race as a whole*. How can the goods of this planet be distributed equitably for all men? (At present, for example, 1 per cent of the U.S. population absorbs 25 percent of consumer goods in America.)

For humans to say that they believe in God, but to fail in duties of stewardship for the entire human race, is to stand in a doubled meaning of the phrase in "bad faith." Thus, one crisis of faith in our time grows out of false faith—belief in an empty God, belief from which justice and love do not flow. Many *purport* to be living in God and God in them. They seem to be, instead, walking idols.

But there is another crisis of faith in our time. It grows out of a total identification of religion with politics. Belief in God is made equivalent to political action. Authentic faith is made

[20] 1 Jn. 1.

[21] Dom Helder Camara, *Revolution Through Peace*, New York, 1971.

[22] Guido Gonella cites Pius XII: ". . . goods, created by God for all mankind, should be equally available to all, according to the principles of justice and charity." And Aquinas: "Temporal things given to man by God are his as regards possession, but as regards use they are not only his but also others'" (*S.T.* 2–2, 32, 5, ad2). *The Papacy and World Peace*, London, 1945.

identical with reformist or revolutionary action. Belief in God is politicized from the point of view of the future; that is to say, from the Left. A seesaw effect is thus created with the politicization of belief nourished by the Right.

There is no way of separating politics from religion. Every attempt to preach "the pure gospel" passes an implicit judgment on the powers of this world. Either it reinforces or it weakens the structural injustice of inherited arrangements. The Right legitimizes what is; the Left legitimizes the future. Every act of legitimation involves an appeal to a transcendent order, a higher law, in the name of which one might give one's own life. It is as though Left and Right seized opposite arms of God and tried to pull God in their direction. (One modern word for God is "History" written with a capital "H.")

A more profound political theology would, however, appeal to a God beyond the God of politics, a God under whose judgment the humans who struggle in history on opposite sides are still humans. On neither side do humans become pigs or beasts, even when their actions are inhumane. Even the Nazis, despite their chosen bestiality, remained human beings; corrupted, wanton, cruel, to be opposed to the death, but humans.

The total politicization of life, whether in the name of the Right or in the name of the Left, is not and cannot be Christian. A sign distinguishing authentic from inauthentic Christianity is a steady insistence upon treating one's political opponents, despite provocation, as human beings. An evangelical injunction effectively bars the total politicization of Christianity: "Love your enemies. Do good to those who hate you." Christianity has in the past assumed both conservative and revolutionary forms, and both sorts of forms are subject to corruption. Conservative or revolutionary, the Christian is committed to a God who transcends political factions and who judges all men equally.

A sign of authenticity in Christian political partisanship is the resolute avoidance of description through moral abstraction.[23] To picture one's political opponents as representing Evil, Injustice, Death is to presume to speak in the name of God, and thus to be guilty of idolatry. To call one's friends and fellow partisans the forces of Conscience, Goodness, Decency, Justice, Progress is to presume too much.

The temptation to abstraction is, of course, inherent in action. Simple, absolute moral appeals catalyze urgency and boldness. They provide a "charismatic" shorthand. It is necessary, however, to test charismata; not all are genuine or, in Christian terms, of God. Napoleon, Hitler, Mussolini, "Papa Doc" Duvalier and many other passionate leaders in history have had charisma.

It is one thing for men of mature age to speak in abstractions of forces of Life and Death, Justice and Injustice. The effect upon young persons in their twenties, the age of moral abstraction, the age of good soldiers and good militants on all sides of every passion, is devastating. Young people do not have a complicated and dense experience of life. They receive abstractions purely and simply. To say to them that the government of the United States has become an empire of Death is to coerce their consciences. For who, faced with absolute evil and being of tender conscience, can do other than throw his life into the wheels?

What does belief in God entail at the present time? We work in a dark night, each uncertain of his own judgments.[24] Many feel a great need to purify themselves, to give meaning and clarity to their lives. Many seek a strong, clear commitment. Sectarian bitterness is intensified. Many daily thank God that

[23] Cp. Albert Camus, *The Rebel,* New York, 1956.

[24] Daniel Berrigan's latest title is appropriately called *The Dark Night of the Resistance,* New York, 1971.

they are not as reactionary, or merely reformist, as other men. The ascendant pose is "lefter than thou."

Some good men, like the Berrigans, are moved by intense political-religious passions to cut a clear swathe through history. They oblige others to reflect and to take a stand. But what stand ought others to take? What does belief in God entail, especially for the young?

First, the invisible religion must everywhere be unmasked, not least in the churches. It is a most powerful religion, deeply embedded in our economic and social structure.

Second, the traditional American turn to the primacy of immediate experience, to sectarianism, to conversion, radicalization, and revivalism must also be transcended. There is not much point, either theological or political, to cycles of over-organization and rebellion against organization. This division is itself a main pillar of the invisible religion.

Third, the planetary situation of the young people of the United States must be grasped: their incomparable wealth, power, skills; their responsibility for all their brothers and sisters. How can any young people claim to believe in God if they do not labor to effect an equitable sharing of the planet's resources?

Fourth, to effect an equitable sharing of the world's resources, not out of charity but out of the strictest sense of justice, present arrangements of world power and interest must be altered. That is to say, political action is required. Such action is required, not least, in the United States.

Fifth, political judgments are necessarily contingent, ambiguous, and full of risk. Those whose training is theological or moral commonly make simplistic political judgments; they tend to be absolutist and fanatical. They often wrestle against themselves in order not to perceive the world through lenses of moral abstraction.

Sixth, persons in power in bureaucratic democracies become implicated in special corruptions different from those involved in other political systems. Abuses of power and trust in a democracy are not as open and flagrant as those in a dictatorship, but they may be just as pervasive and efficacious. They need to be unmasked and effectively opposed.

Seventh, the actual workings of power and interest in bureaucratic democracies do not coincide with the propaganda about the virtues of democracies. Neither an informed public opinion, nor "good men" in office, nor "a constituency of conscience" are strong enough in the balance against entrenched powers and interests.[25] Thus, a theological criticism which concentrates on "awakening" individual consciences and raising levels of "awareness" is like a theology of good sentiments and warm feelings: it does not go deep enough to be authentic.

Eighth, it is not at all a plain fact that an equitable distribution of the world's resources is an historical possibility. That requires an act of faith beyond the act of faith in God. Belief in human progress and human perfectibility is important to the Left; belief in tragic brokenness and incompleteness is important to the Right. Young middle class Americans today have grown up in such private contexts that their expectations of justice, fairness, beauty, and love are unprecedented in history—except that they are so typically American. Robert Jay Lifton, for example, writes eloquently of "a new history;"[26] in an earlier America, it was "a new world," "a new paradise," "a new Eden."

[25] See the criticism of electoral politics made by Garry Wills in *Nixon Agonistes*, Boston, 1970, pp. 434–455.
[26] *The Atlantic Monthly,* October, 1969.

There is still the pursuit of the little green light beckoning through the mist.

Ninth, Christian theology holds that men can and must make progress toward building up God's Kingdom, "on earth as it is in heaven." As distinct from some other world religions, Christianity places upon men responsibility for the shaping of history. On the other hand, Christian theology does not anticipate the advent of a Kingdom of justice, truth, freedom, and love on this earth. We work toward it and are judged accordingly; but its fulfillment is neither in our hands nor promised to us.

Tenth, politics is not the whole of life.[27] A wholly politicized life makes a caricature of a man; it, so to speak, Nixonizes him. Politics lies in the field of earthly, non-transcendent, temporal, and ambivalent arrangements. There has never been, is not now, and never will be a political order exhaustively representative of the Gospels. One cannot ask more of politics than it can give. It is neither food nor drink for the soul. It is an instrument of, but not the substance of, the building of a world of justice, freedom, truth and love. City hall, congress, and "movement" are to humanism what chancery, curia, and progressivism are to church: in neither case the heart of the matter.

Eleventh, the need of countless human beings on this planet for food, income, justice, liberty, and self-expression is enormous. It is, some argue, no greater than it ever was; the difference is that we are far more conscious of it. (Many young people do not recognize that conditions in Europe and America two centuries ago were as economically oppressive as those still borne by millions elsewhere.) On the other hand, the growth of the United States as a world power coincides with the growth of technology

[27] See Peter Berger, in Berger and Richard Neuhaus, *Movement and Revolution, op. cit.*

in alleviating some human problems (lowering death rates, for example) and in adding to others (impersonal and vast methods of military control). As the first technological world power, the United States is a major part of the network of economic control upon the planet. Moreover, in the United States itself, centers of economic power have disproportionate power over internal and external political life.[28]

That is to say, twelfth, that freedom and justice are under economic siege both in the United States and on the planet as a whole. Economic "principalities and powers" hold us, to some degree, in thrall.

3. Belief in God

Conclusions from these twelve presuppositions are not easy to state succinctly or simply. The question of belief in God is not *identical* with the question of political stance. Belief in God transcends any and all political positions. On the other hand, belief in God is *not separable* from political positions. Political choices are ways of expressing in concrete institutional history the sense of reality, story, and symbols to which one is committed.[29] It is the responsibility of theologians to draw out the hidden connections between religious choices and political choices, so as to minimize "bad faith." The slogan carved in stone over the portals of many parochial schools, "For God and Country," for example, fails to suggest the probability that national power and the Gospels will very often be at variance.

In order to believe in God, must one be a revolutionary? We might imagine a person deeply committed to the view that

[28] See, among others, G. William Domhoff, *Who Rules America?*, Englewood Cliffs, N.J., 1967.
[29] See my *Story in Politics*, New York, 1970.

178

civilization is gossamer and that a breakdown in mutual trust is always near at hand. In his eyes, riot, hostility, rage, and terror are always just around the corner. His political views, consequently, tend to emphasize the importance of authority, law, order and stability. He concedes that there are many bitter injustices in the social order; in fact, that is his very starting point: injustice is endemic to social orders, indeed endemic to individual humans. Men are inherently rapacious, untrustworthy, stiffnecked and fickle. In a word, one can imagine a vivid belief in God wedded to a profound and chastened political conservatism, without bad faith.[30]

One can just as easily imagine belief in God wedded to political radicalism; and—to complicate the matter—one may imagine the union of God and Left as a union in "bad faith." For example, a clergyman loses his faith in the transcendent, in the sacraments, in his own sacred role, in the Word of God. He discovers the human potential movement, or the anti-war movement, feels an internal liberation, experiences a new kind of enlightenment, and finds a new identity and new scope for action. Now whenever he says "God" he means either a feeling of community between people or fidelity to a political program. "God" is reduced to a transaction between humans. But the clergyman goes on using "God" language for emotions, purposes, intentions and activities that are exhaustively described by others in a secular language which does not refer to God. It is quite possible that the clergyman is engaged in "mystification" if not in outright "bad faith."[31]

[30] Peter Berger, a conservative, and Richard Neuhaus, a radical, evince political disagreement while in theological "good faith." See their *Movement and Revolution, op. cit.*

[31] See the caricature by Dorothy Rabinowitz, "The Activist Cleric," *Commentary* (September, 1970), pp. 81–83.

There is a difference between saying that to feed the hungry, etc., is a *sign* that one loves God and saying that such acts are *identical with* love of God.[32] To show the difference, two opposite contexts must be used. In one context, the argument is that belief in God refers to some special transcendent, private, "supernatural" experience; the emphasis is on how *different* the believer is from the humanist. In that context, I note how *in action* and *in experience* both believer and humanist may be indistinguishable, although the *interpretation* each gives his (her) actions and experiences differs.[33]

In a second context, however, the argument is that belief in God is exhausted by actions and experiences of a certain humanistic sort; the emphasis is on *the identity* of the believer and the humanist. In that context, I note that the interpretation one gives one's actions and experiences *in the long run* affects their character.[34] Specifically, the interpretation according to which when I feed the hungry and the like, God is living in me and I in God, adds a profound dimension to my identity, to my connections to the past and the future, and above all to the sense in which I am not my own master. Autonomy and theonomy both differ from heteronomy; but they are not equal to each other.[35]

Revolutionary activity, therefore, is not the equivalent of believing in God. But it often is a legitimate and powerful expression of belief in God. What are some of the conditions

[32] Karl Rahner asserts this identity in "Reflections on the Unity of the Love of Neighbor and the Love of God," *Theological Investigations VI,* Baltimore, 1969, pp. 231–249.

[33] The argument of *Belief and Unbelief.*

[34] The argument of "The Odd Logic of Theism and Non-Theism," *A Time to Build,* New York, 1967, pp. 60–69.

[35] See J. Maritain, *Integral Humanism,* New York, 1968, pp. 27–34; also Paul Tillich, *The Protestant Era,* Chicago, 1962, pp. 44 ff; 55 ff.

under which revolutionary activity becomes such an expression? One watershed is, of course, the conviction that such activity makes the human condition more expressive of justice, truth, freedom and community, and not less so. Revolutionaries and reformers are often enemies of each other, each believing that the other causes more harm than good. Conservatives commonly believe that the present, however unjust, is more expressive of justice, truth, freedom, and community than the future aspired to by reformers and revolutionaries.

There is, in a word, a realm which is not "beyond" politics, since it of necessity must express itself in and through concrete political choices, but which "transcends" politics. It is the realm in which men, of whatever diverse political persuasion and concrete judgment, are brothers. It is the realm of the dynamic, attracting term of human development: unity as one human race. It is the eschaton already active in our midst, not a promise merely, but a dynamic principle of communion.

This principle of communion must be testified to not in words but in action. It cannot be testified to by those whose political choices are masked, hidden, unexamined, theologically unconscious; for they are living in "bad faith." Theological consciousness is not complete until it includes political consciousness. For political action is the basic structural modality through which belief in the communion of the human race expresses itself. Christians must elaborate the political consequences of their personal and communal theological positions; they cannot pretend that political expression and theological position are separate and independent. Since the same person is at once a theological and a political animal, integrity demands a conscious connection between his theology and his politics.

There are, however, many theologies and many political positions. Sectarianism and fanaticism are models neither for

181

the kingdom of God nor for a humane political society. On the other hand, the danger with too managerial a pluralism—a benign *laissez-faire*—is that it dissipates both political and theological passion. Doctrinal pluralism is a basic tenet of the invisible religion. The good fruit of such a position is tolerance, variety, and wider insight. A corrupt fruit is the one-dimensionality of the merely practical, the evasion of radical differences, the homogenization of everybody. It is in such a sense that Garry Wills calls Richard Nixon "the last liberal."[36]

We cannot in conscience speak of belief in God today without at the same time speaking of politics. We have an obligation to speak each in his (her) own voice, elucidating our theology and its connections to our politics, and obliging our associates to do the same. The fact that no one of us should be coerced, morally or physically, into a theology or into a politics that do not express our own inmost convictions does not mean that we should not argue passionately. To believe that each person is free is not to believe that each person is correct. Nor is it to believe that matters which cannot be univocally settled are matters of indifference. The passion of believing oneself correct and being willing to die for one's views has both theological and political importance of the highest conceivable order. Such a passion is saved from fanaticism by the effective recognition that other good men hold other views with equal passion and equal right.

Human beings on this planet are, and ought to be, diverse. Animated, civil conversation is an alternative to murder. The construction of a social order in which such conversation is an ordinary exercise is the goal toward which belief in God commits us.

[36] *Op. cit.*

182

14

Bringing Up Children Catholic

But how do we bring up our children? That is where every theoretical question comes down to earth. Thinking is not a personal activity; it is communal, and it *will* be transmitted. What, then, shall we transmit?

Children come to experience fresh and impressionable; and there is no way to be neutral with them. Whatever they experience, *that* becomes part of them. I have heard of psychoanalysts who kept Grimm's fairy tales and all the other classical fables about monsters and witches, ghosts and gore, away from their children. They wished their children's imaginations not to be "haunted." But into those empty spaces (so I have heard) swept demons of sadism and masochism invented, of necessity, by the children themselves—demons more literal, less poetic, more destructive by far. The imagination cannot stand bare. And the inner life of children is full of fears, terrors, insecurities. Children have a most acute sense of fragility, death, and the absurd. At any moment, their instincts recognize, life could be taken from them. Even the drain in the bathtub may threaten to suck them down: down, down, down to nothingness.

Children have a profound need for guidance as to what is real, what stories to try to live out with their lives, what symbols to use to structure the overwhelming floods of experience that pour in upon them every day. Moreover, our children grow up in a world in which their consciousness will be affected by the impact of many other cultures besides our own. As we have seen, even a theologian can no longer stand, in Tillich's phrase, "within the theological circle." Like everyone else, the theologian must do more than seek an understanding of the faith handed down to her by her parents or by her particular own religious community. The alert human today finds that she learns wisdom from many cultures and many communities besides the one into which she was born. From a Christian standpoint, this turn of events is not, upon reflection, surprising. The same Word in whom, by whom, and with whom all things were made manifests himself in two ways: within the concrete historical community of his selection, and in all the communities of man, who equally spring from his creative hand and who mirror back to God his dappled, manysided, and not at all finite glory.

1. The New Direction: Down and In

There is, however, an understandable failure of nerve among many Christians as they experience the corruptions embedded deep within their own historical traditions and the freshly discovered power and holiness of religious traditions not their own. Why should anyone be a Christian at all? And why, in particular, would anyone care to belong to a church as bureaucratically encrusted and poorly led as the Roman Catholic church?

Perhaps (to recapitulate) the first answer is that that is where we find ourselves. We are the Catholic people. We are no other. For better or worse, there lie the deep and ancient roots of our identity, which it is difficult to shed. Every day people "leave the Church," and every day the inner erosion of that imagination and instinct which constitute belonging to a people proceeds

184

a little further in innumerable other modern persons. Still, those in whom a Catholic imagination and instinct are strong cannot escape by leaving the institution or by trying to make themselves modern. The "invisible religion" of American society has lost as much of its credibility as has the church.

The second answer, however, is more affirmative. Many of us remain Catholic, finally, out of a conviction that the route toward becoming planetary humans does not pass by way of the universal, the general, the abstract. It does not proceed by the route of some universal Reason in each person, by which all persons are brothers and are one. There is no such universal Reason; and it is not in and through Reason that men of the diverse human communities become one. Rather, the route by which we each become planetary men passes by way of our own autobiographies: the deeper we search through time and memory for our uttermost sources, the nearer we come to all other men.

The unity of mankind is not founded upon some future image of a universal Reason in which all, overcoming their particularity, will be happy to share. The unity of mankind does not lie "up ahead." It lies already within us, in a kind of primal memory, in the destiny each human shares of discovering and inventing who she is and what story she shall tell with her life. The unity of mankind lies in the originating Word which each culture, each person, echoes in fragmented form. Only when every fragment is heard in its own particular, authentic tone does the whole human echo of the infinite Word approach infinity. Many variations are required if infinity is to be even remotely suggested.

The route to the unity of the human race, in a word, is by way of each of us going as deeply as each can into his own tradition. There is no shortcut. There is no general, universal, cosmopolitan, completely "open" (that is, indeterminate) way. There is only the way of the concrete, here and now, *us,* me—as we are, who we are, with all our limitations.

The questions, "Who am I?" and "Who are we?", the two primary theological questions, lead us into limitless depths. They lead us into a kind of knowing which is more like ignorance than like knowing. They lead us, paradoxically, not into egocentricity but into community with every other human under this same hot sun, under these same stars. They lead us, finally, to political consciousness.

Until the last part of the twentieth century, men were relatively powerless to change their societies and social structures. Economies, governments, and families possessed remarkable stability. Today, too, social and political institutions are of breathtaking solidity. But we are able to imagine, at least, that almost any part of any social structure might be different from what it is. We are aware of other possibilities. Social structures have been "demystified"—our attitude toward them has changed. We imagine at least (and perhaps we are grievously in error) that everything is subject to change; everything may be reconceived and re-designed. The consequence is that every theological term we use—faith, despair, conscience, person, community—is now understood to carry with it a social and political imperative. What social structure best expresses our theological convictions? What social structure most faithfully expresses who we think we are (ought to be)?

This shift in our conception of social order is overwhelming. No longer do people merely accept their social order as a given, as an inevitable factor with which they must make some realistic peace, or against which make some tragically doomed protest. On the contrary, Americans (at least) are easily made to feel guilty for the social institutions they find in their possession. The conviction has gained ground that social institutions *ought* to express our identity faithfully; whereas, in times past, it was always assumed that identity was something one worked out in and around and between the rather fixed and inevitably evil institutions in which one happened to find oneself.

This new American consciousness of the malleability of institutions is in part meretricious, shallow, and all-too-American. There is, on the other hand, a profound insight hidden within it. The human perspective is, at last, planetary. All men together experienced the landings on the moon. The astronauts looked back on the one whole planet. The economic and military conflicts of Indochina, Latin America, the Near East, and Pakistan reverberate on those mysterious networks which now bind all our destinies together. It is true then—it is really true—that we must think more carefully than our forebears were obliged to do about the social, political and economic correlatives of our theological assertions. The seriousness of our vision of humanity is tested not by what we say but by what we do. Exactly in proportion as we are free citizens, we are responsible for what our nation does. *We* are responsible.

The truth is, however, that we are not entirely free. During World War II, Jean-Paul Sartre argued as dramatically as any philosopher ever has in defense of the ultimate, unshirkable freedom of the person. Each of us is, he said, "condemned to freedom." In recent years, his investigations into the structures and context of social institutions have led him to see that the margin of freedom within which the human being defines his own unique identity is inexpressibly small.[1] At every point in our psyche, we are conditioned by social forces in operation long

[1] See his *A Search for Method*, New York, 1968, and "An Interview with Sartre," *New York Review of Books* (March 26, 1970).

before we became aware of their operations. To the questions, "Who am I?" and "Who are we?", the theologian quite properly adds another: "Under what institutions do I live?"

In the last three years, many Catholics who had gathered great hope from the Second Vatican Council—especially from the discussions on "the Church in the Modern World"—pushed off as it were from the barque of Peter and gave more and more of their energies to the needs of the modern world. The situation of American politics was unusually open to them. The struggle for civil rights and the war in Vietnam generated some of the most explicitly moral and religious political turmoil in American history. The transfer of religious zeal into political channels was so natural and unobstructed as to be almost effortless.

Catholics, moreover, with a tradition of resistance to mere pragmatism and even to the dominant liberal ethos of the WASP establishment, soon found their own peculiar contributions much in demand. Their liturgical instincts were suited to the new "theater of the streets." The high visibility and moral prestige of their priests and religious were dramatic assets. The aura of surprising change generated by Vatican II made Catholics, wherever they appeared, symbols of ferment and vessels of hope. (The symbolism was not always flattering; it sometimes took the form: "If *they* can change, anyone can . . . the N.A.M., the A.M.A., city hall . . .")

It was not by accident that a Mario Savio gave the transcendent, unpragmatic touch to the Berkeley uprising of 1964; that a tough Father Groppi led the most hard-nosed of all black movements in the North; that a Eugene McCarthy, whose metaphors were almost entirely—and deliberately—parochial Catholic, was the Senator who put his neck on the line before anyone dreamt that Lyndon Johnson might withdraw; that the

Kennedys awakened a part of the American imagination that no WASP politician could ever reach; or that the vivid picture of Phil and Dan Berrigan concelebrating around the flaming bin of Catonsville should so have touched the soul of our times. The age was ready for a specifically Catholic politics; such Catholics as these were ready when the call came.

But after this great turn to politics these last few years, what next? Unless I am mistaken, the time of accusation and agitation is over. Now again it is a time for quiet growth, in the way a forest grows. We have gone as far as we could go with the big push and the big breakthrough. What needs to be done in the future will be done less through the press, less through demonstrations, less through threats of various kinds. It will be done more through the engendering of quiet interior strength; through persuasion, through example; through bold witness and leadership. I do not mean to exclude any activities from some sort of list of what "should" be done; I am only trying to put into words what I suspect will occur.

America is a land quick to promote restlessness, reform through public relations, and the confrontation model of political action: our sense of political courage often has all the subtlety of *High Noon*. The most accessible American passion is guilt: we love to play on one another's guilt feelings. The most widespread American style is moral indignation. We are perhaps the only people in history who do not believe that original sin especially afflicts officials: we are genuinely shocked to hear that persons in authority have lied, or suppressed information, or acted unjustly. Try telling an Italian that his government has lied to him. "*Eh beh!* And for three thousand years." Finally, Americans are a people whose orientation is not tragic but pathetic. We expect innocence and happiness, and when anything goes wrong we feel unjustly treated, like *victims*. The Peace Movement, for example, at times alternates between the manipulation of guilt feelings, outbreaks of moral indignation, and expression of how badly we have all been victimized.

Any successful movement to change the American character and the structure of American institutions, must, of necessity, break this cycle of traditional American emotions. We cannot go on forever shuttling back and forth between crass hucksters and passionate revivalists. (Who succeed, incidentally, by borrowing from each other. The hucksters learn oily piety; the preachers learn how to hold the crowds. Lyndon Johnson as preacher; Bill Coffin and Philip Berrigan as operators; Billy Graham as the great American synthesis.)

That is why I feel in my bones that the fruitful direction for the future is *inner, down:* the gaining of personal depth, speech that comes from the pit of the stomach and goes to the pit of the stomach, endurance of what Daniel Berrigan is just now calling "the dark night." How do we bring up children prepared for an inauthentic and shallow society? How do we lead them to discover depths in themselves by which to endure until a better time?

The sacraments are meant to perform such work. The liturgy is intended as objective instruction in the descent into death, darkness, the Red Sea, and at some unspecified time emergence into life. The liturgy is not primarily a matter of relevance, or entertainment, or good group relations. It is primarily mystery, tragedy, a community of suffering, a token of courage, a pledge that whoever lays down his life for honesty, courage, freedom, and community has not misjudged what is central in human history: has, in fact, sided with the springs of life and regeneration, whose continuance seems often so precarious.

2. Bringing Up Children Catholic

I wish I knew how we ought to teach children these things. The structure of childhood itself, however, is on our side. Those whose prejudice runs toward "enlightenment" are inclined to believe that children are essentially good, unspoiled, innocent and reasonable; it is society that corrupts them. But the fact is that being born social is part of being born at all. No child born into this world escapes, even from its time in the womb, the corruption of being human. The nervousness, repressed anger, fears, hostilities, anxieties of the parents—as well as their tenderness, their desire to be good, their courage—radiate in the blood that feeds the foetus in the womb, the air the child breathes once born.

We may, then, speak much more frankly to our children of death, evil and corruption than the enlightened would have us do. As Kurt Vonnegut suggests in *Mother Night,* there are no toys sufficiently sadistic, cruel, or absurd to prepare a child for what he will face later in life. We do a disservice to children by surrounding them with innocence, a conspiracy of silence and superficial happiness. They know that life is unfair: why else would sibling rivalry be so intense? They know that life is absurd: they have to adjust to the moods, the language, the comings and goings of their parents—none of which initially makes sense to them. They know that life is precarious and cruel—why else would they be seized by such total horrors, such total panics, at sudden noises or threatening faces?

Moreover, celebrations and rituals in the home feed the children's imagination with symbols by which to interpret cruel or mean things that happen every day, but which the child is sometimes supposed not to notice. Our children were deeply affected by Judas in *Jesus Christ Superstar* and by the lashing

191

given Jesus. It is not as if they hadn't already experienced betrayal; it is not as if they don't know the cruel ridicule and even physical pounding little children (like adults) administer to one another. Dramatizations of envy, competition, and anger which they encountered in a few extraordinary children's books taught them to put into words emotions they had already confusedly felt.

In medieval paintings, children are usually depicted not as children but as miniature adults, even in dress and attitude. The insight is not a bad one. The complexity of children's emotions is overwhelming: the more one helps them to distinguish the variety of conflicts they actually feel, the more one is amazed.

Inventing stories and fables to help give tongue to experiences is, then, a major road toward structuring the inner life of children. A short supply of imaginative materials will leave their experiences mute, confused, and flat. Here is where Christian education was so successful in the past: vivid ceremonies, sights, smells, fears, joys, disciplines, dramatizations, pictures, stories. In the name of enlightenment, the rationalistic spoke of all these elements as superstition and prejudice. And what is the result of an upbringing as resolutely and ascetically cognitive as one can make it? Sterility, alienation, one-dimensionality, an enormous thirst for the power of the imagination.

The family is the locus *par excellence* for instructing the imagination. The nuclear family is an impoverished version of the family, to be sure: it was the marvellous characters of the extended family—crotchety and doting grandparents, eccentric uncles, perceptive aunts—who peopled the imaginations of children in bygone years. Today, the minds of children are peopled with television cartoons and characters.

Moreover, even the modern family style, suburban or urban, is impoverishing. The family is more like a service station than

192

an imaginative center; more like a pragmatic living arrangement than like a focal point of how to structure one's own attitudes toward life. Many children seem to expect to learn about how to structure reality, not from their parents, but from their peers, their travel, their movies, their books, their music. Parents are in a weaker position vis-à-vis the outlooks of their children than ever before.

Still, if what the parents have communicated to children opens their imagination to the realities corroborated by their later experience—to the difficulties inherent in maintaining their integrity, to habits of heart and intuition that enable them to make flexible but astute moral judgments in situations in which there are no rules, to strength during the tragedy and absurdity of so much that will come their way—the children, whatever identity they end up inventing for themselves, will have met the human situation as it is. The prejudice in America is to "see the bright side of things," to pretend that evils do not exist or will yield easily to reason and good will. Parents who arm their children against this pollyanna prejudice, who prepare them to be tough and persevering, have given their children a priceless gift.

I am trying to suggest that a Christian imagination is more in tune with the way the world is than the story of progress and Reason told by the Enlightenment. But the imagination cannot be instructed didactically, as if life were a set of lessons. The imagination is subtle, deeply in touch with emotions and sensitivities. Feeling one's way toward attunement with a child's imagination is a delicate activity. The eyes of children "light up" when an image joins experiences they know; otherwise, they are dutifully or restlessly bored. Words are not so important to children; often they get the point without needing to verbalize it or hear more words about it.

193

A family eucharist—breaking of bread, passing of a cup—is often more telling to their imagination than attendance at church. A large nail passed hand to hand, a thorn, says more than many words about how cruel men were to Jesus—and often are. But no special gimmick does the trick. Children—and parents—differ. Genuineness is everything. What do *you* believe? That is the question most disconcerting to all of us as parents. What do we genuinely hold, in our imagination and our instincts, as well as in tutored memory and word?

One criterion is helpful to keep in mind. Whatever we tell children, is life really like that? We don't want to picture life for them as more pretty or more reasonable than it is. Neither do we want to inhibit them, or cripple them with fear. There is death, and there is resurrection. In our culture, it is important to stress, the partisans of joy and hope and optimism and new beginnings join hands with the partisans of guilt. Man is good, they assert, and *if only* . . . if only we overthrew his corrupt institutions *then* lions would lie down with lambs. Christianity is converted into a society of cheer and futurology. Hoping too much of men in the abstract, they heap too much guilt on men in the concrete.

It was concrete humans Jesus died for, and called others to suffer for and die, without promising that the good kingdom will be achieved on earth. The cross is a sign of the absurdity of life, from which painful creativity is wrung.

We in America need to know that the world belongs to the prince of darkness; is contested yet; and that the forces of that invisible religion which is so powerful and dominant—the religion whose monuments are Dallas, O'Hare terminal, musak, glass skyscrapers, 747's and anti-personnel bombs that shred all human flesh within a radius of one hundred yards—that the forces of the invisible religion are the real enemy both of

Christianity and of men in our time. The invisible religion is pragmatism, utility, relevance, action now, image, loneliness, the individual; and its newest offshoot is instant revolution, instant intimacy, instant dissent, instant resistance, instant militance. So many people do not know how to find what their own instincts and emotions and judgments would have them do. They wait for someone to make them feel guilty, to move them, and then they join the cause. Conversions, while intense, are not deep. What is "in" today will be "out" tomorrow. The dogmatic force of the invisible religion is concentrated in one single imperative: "Be where the action is"; "Be where it's at."

There is a difference between being a good steward who brings out from his treasure new things and old, exactly appropriate to the circumstance, and merely being with it. That distinction depends upon an inner life deep enough and rich enough not to be surprised, not to be caught without resources, and not, either, to be dismayed when one stands empty-handed and without resources. The difference, in a word, is practice in poverty of spirit.

What are the deep, enduring values of the Catholic people? They are such things as poverty of spirit; the dark night; emptiness; solitude; community with all eras, all times, all peoples; a certain cynicism regarding power and its uses; a profound awareness of the physical reality of evil and the prevailing stench of inauthenticity; a joy in creation and its simple fruits—the beads of sweat on a cold stein of beer in July; internal merriment because, despite everything, God is good.

No revolution worthy of the name is built without some such attitudes; no revolution will make such attitudes expendable.

On the other hand, the Catholic is committed to language and symbolism in the eucharist according to which he pledges himself to stand as one grain of wheat in a single bread, one drop of juice in a single wine, one brother or one sister to an entire planetary race. The eucharist commits us to a politics of civil conversation, of peace, of justice, of freedom, of truth—and to the invention of institutions appropriate to such a pledge. We do not deceive ourselves that we live under such institutions now, in the United States of America or elsewhere. The eucharist which we celebrate condemns every day the lies, injustices, and grinding misuse of power and wealth for which the people of the United States are, if free, then responsible. The eucharist condemns these evils not in order to make us feel guilty, or morally indignant, or full of self-pity for our helplessness. It condemns them in order to show us truthfully who we are, far less good than we pretend, and to call us out upon that long and far from completed pilgrimage toward the political reconstruction of this planet. We shall not be able, finally, to construct on earth a kingdom of love, a kingdom of justice, a kingdom of truth, a kingdom of liberty. But it is toward that goal that we are obliged to work with every energy we have.

The Protestant style in such work is often that of preachment and the manipulation of guilt; the Jewish style is often that of alienation and dissent. The Catholic style is, on the one hand, dramatic and liturgical; and, on the other hand, quietly cynical, modest, steady and slow. Catholics are particularly good at accepting the necessities of power, the slow and ugly tasks of organizing and administrating, the messiness of hard decisions, and the inevitability of "dirty hands." We did not have a long line of renaissance popes for nothing.

That is why I am hopeful that the slow, fumbling work of organizing, raising money, finding concrete issues, relentlessly pressing, patiently proceeding will not disturb Catholics now that the romantic period is at an end. This is what life is like. Grubby, slow, difficult, earthy, grit in the wheels, snafus.

196

Catholics are the people of concrete detail, the people not so much of saints or even flamboyant sinners but of ordinary sinners, the people of ordinary parents in ordinary places, as they are, the people, in Lincoln's words, God made so many of. Those who have vocations of leadership do well to trust that people, to ask more of them than has been asked, to organize them, and to get them moving again. They are a pilgrim people. They are better educated and more sophisticated now than at any age in history.

Our specific mission in the United States is to give tongue to the silent majority, to voice the pain and agony felt by the hard hats, to listen to the anguish of the grandchildren of immigrants from non-English-speaking lands. These are our people. Most of them are Catholics. Most are despised by many in the educated classes, not understood by liberals or by conservatives either. They are the tongueless ones. Their pain is great. The decade of the seventies is liable to be their decade. The Catholic vote in the United States is at present the swing vote between progress and reaction. It gives promise of being a base from which one could redefine all the issues of American politics.

A lot remains to be done: internally and in our political structures. The people from whom we spring, the Catholic people, has unique strengths in both directions. The more worthy we are of our ancestors, the more proudly our children will continue the slow and trackless pilgrimage, bringing to other peoples on this planet the witness of a unique and valuable style.

Index

199